HOW TO PROFIT
FROM THE
SAVINGS AND LOAN
CRISIS

Michael J. Stich

by

Michael J. Stich

How to Profit from the Savings and Loan Crisis
Copyright © 1989
by Michael J. Stich

All rights reserved. No portion of this book may be reproduced or used in any format, by photocopying, recording, or by any information storage or retrieval system, or by any other form or manner whatsoever, without prior written consent of the publisher. Reviewers may, however, quote brief passages in connection with reviews prepared for magazines, newspapers, or broadcasts.

Published by Wilchester Publishing Company
          1407 W. Brooklake Ct., Ste. 200
          P.O. Box 820874
          Houston, Texas 77282-0874
          (713) 496-0788

ISBN: 0-9622730-0-7
Library of Congress Catalog Card Number: 89-50593
Printed in the United States of America
by D. Armstrong Co., Inc.
Houston, Texas

CONTENTS

TABLES

PREFACE

This book was written to satisfy the need for a business person's guide to the savings and loan crisis. It attempts to relate how the Federal Savings and Loan Insurance Corporation (FSLIC) has battled the thrift industry's insolvencies and how the Federal Deposit Insurance Corporation (FDIC) might help. As a result of thrift failures, over $120 billion of foreclosed real estate must be managed and sold at huge taxpayer losses. Unlimited business potential exists for the private sector to supply goods and services for repossessed real estate. Investment opportunities abound, whether the FSLIC, the FDIC, or a partnership of the two disposes of the properties.

The savings and loan industry has had a traditional purpose. Without the thrift industry, the American dream of owning a home might not have been possible. Thrift history is reviewed to understand why Congress embraced savings and loans with favorable legislation. The roles of the Federal Home Loan Bank Board (FHLBB), the District Banks, the FSLIC, and the FDIC are outlined. The Federal Home Loan Bank System has complex interrelationships that are extremely difficult to dissolve. A straightforward discussion of recent FSLIC liquidation strategy leads to the Federal Asset Disposition Association (FADA) dispute. A chapter is dedicated to FDIC history, failed bank resolution methodology, and bank asset sales.

Readers will be aided by the book's deliberate intention to simplify. A chapter is devoted to how the FSLIC really sells assets. The policies and procedures of FSLIC asset sales are defined. Highlights of FSLIC institutional asset management philosophy introduce the step-by-step process of how to purchase FSLIC assets. Investors, contractors, and vendors of goods and services will discover who and where to telephone for FSLIC and FDIC business. Convenient appendices list important FSLIC, FDIC, FADA, and District Bank addresses and telephone numbers. A "plain English" glossary defines the thrift industry, real estate, and disposition terms utilized in the manuscript.

The book's closing explores legislative proposals for the thrift industry's future. Although many studies and recommendations have surfaced, the fundamental problem—foreclosed, distressed real estate—still must be resolved. Private industry can participate in tremendous opportunities. This book intends to show each reader how to profit from the savings and loan crisis while helping solve our nation's distressed real estate problems.

INTRODUCTION

Before the 1830s, Americans patiently saved and paid cash for their homes. To create a source of funds, home financing societies and mutual savings banks developed. These societies enabled their members to purchase homes on credit. In 1932 the Federal Home Loan Bank Board (FHLBB) System was created to provide access to a national pool of credit. The National Housing Act of 1934 established federal deposit insurance through the Federal Savings and Loan Insurance Corporation (FSLIC) as a result of the massive savings account losses and foreclosures of the 1929 crash and subsequent depression. Since that legislation, there have been years of stability and steady growth along with remarkable successes and prominent failures.

In the early 1900s, Congress understood the importance of the housing industry and its considerable influence on the national economy. By creating the FHLBB System, the thrift industry received special rights and privileges to aid the home building business. Through the FHLBB, Congress granted extraordinary tax benefits to savings and loans. In return, savings and loans offered long-term, flat-rate home mortgages and noncompetitive passbook deposits. Home mortgage interest rate exposure created thrift institution balance sheet risk. During national credit crunches, savings and loans experienced serious income deficiencies.

In the 1970s, Congressional actions began to change directions. Thrift institutions no longer served the housing industry as intended. Savings and loans often became obstacles to Congressional desires. New federal regulations, although intended to make thrifts more competitive, actually strapped them with higher operating costs. Commercial banks, money market funds, and higher interest rate competition threatened the very existence of the thrift industry. Rising interest rates pushed the cost of funds beyond the savings industry's return on assets. Long-term home mortgages with low, fixed-rates of interest did not justify certificates of deposit paying high, deregulated market rates. By 1982 the savings and loan industry's financial setbacks had successfully blocked individual attempts by thrifts to restructure.

The Garn-St Germain Depository Institutions Act of 1982 was designed to give thrifts new business opportunities to survive. The Act differed from the 1930's reforms by deregulating rather than regulating. Savings institutions gained authority to expand into additional business areas including commercial real estate lending and direct investment in real estate. These investment options, however, relied heavily upon continued rapid inflation and economic growth especially in the oil patch states. State legislatures granted state-chartered thrifts even greater investment authority. Speculation, greed, and fraud combined to severely affect the entire savings industry. Thrifts everywhere were seeking to rebuild depleted capital positions with high yielding assets. The end result was unprofitable non-earning assets.

Financial losses to the FSLIC deposit insurance fund have continued at an astounding pace since 1982. Congress attempted to replenish the FSLIC's insurance fund with the passage of the Competitive Equality Banking Act of 1987 (CEBA). The Act's $10.8 billion bonding authority did not provide sufficient funding to solve the problem. This is especially true as the Southwest real estate markets remain depressed. Problems continue to escalate as other regional markets react to overbuilding.

The total cost of the thrift industry bailout could be more than the combined cost of the World War II Marshall Plan for European recovery and the federal bailouts of Chrysler Corporation, New York City, Lockheed Corporation, and the Penn Central Railroad.

The insolvency of the FSLIC has negatively impacted the entire thrift industry as well as the U.S. economy. Some bankrupt savings associations have been consolidated into healthier thrift organizations. However, the fundamental source of the failures still remains. Loans that become nonperforming assets eventually face foreclosure. The collateral turns into real estate owned (REO) and a drain against thrift earnings. Even if the REO assets are written down to zero book value, holding costs for taxes, insurance, management expertise, and other normal operating expenses continue to accrue. Real estate improvements are not built to remain empty.

Thrift institutions should be complimented on their diligent efforts to deal with distressed properties. However, as history has illustrated, federal regulators, thrift institutions, and banks have had great difficulty performing cost effective asset or property management. The financial industry seldom receives substantial profits from the direct investment in real estate, except for headquarters sales. Money managers can generate more profit by relying upon private sector real estate professionals to manage and dispose of troubled real estate.

A goal of this book is to highlight the history of the thrift industry, reasons for its current crisis, and the importance of private industry's involvement. FSLIC and FDIC policies for the management and disposition of insolvent institutions are presented. The fundamental cause of thrift institution insolvencies is foreclosed REO. Private industry must work with the FSLIC and the FDIC to create stability in the thrift industry. All interested parties must understand thrift history and federal regulatory policy to forge this partnership. In many markets, stability will take years to accomplish. This is due to the billions of dollars lost when regional market values plummeted. The rebirth process must be a joint effort between government, the real estate professions, and private enterprise. FSLIC and FDIC regulatory activity will continue to play a major role in establishing real estate sales prices for years to come. Every American citizen should be alarmed by the eventual cost of the resolution of the FSLIC deposit insurance bankruptcy. As tax-payers, there has never been a more appropriate time for the real estate sector to stand up and be heard. Only active participation will ensure that Congress, the FDIC, and the thrift industry create a solution that will be affordable and realistic for future generations. The answer to the thrift industry dilemma must integrate a working partnership between the FSLIC, the FDIC, thrift institutions, and the private real estate sector.

Chapter 1.

THRIFT INDUSTRY HISTORY

Industry Beginnings

In the early 1800s, if a person wanted to buy a house, he had to borrow funds from family and friends, or save the entire purchase amount. At that time, banks catered solely to large industrial, commercial, and agricultural concerns. Banks did not lend to individuals with small accounts to purchase homes. Consequently, people accumulated savings under their beds and floorboards. The earliest thrift institutions evolved from groups of neighbors. They pooled savings and lent other group members funds to purchase homes.

The first home financing cooperative was organized in Pennsylvania in 1831. The association had 37 members who contributed three dollars each. Members further agreed to deposit three dollars per month until all members obtained the necessary funds. The second cooperative was formed in Brooklyn in 1836. South Carolina boasted the third in 1843.

These early cooperatives charged no interest on loans. Drawings were held to determine the order in which members would receive home loans. Individual members made equal monthly payments until all the original members had purchased homes. The mortgages were then canceled and the cooperative terminated.

As time passed, the associations auctioned loans to the highest bidding members. Eventually, interest was charged on borrowed amounts. As associations grew, emphasis shifted from building new homes to receiving a return on investments. Gradually, the associations moved from members' homes into permanent offices. Professional staffs allowed new members to join and invest in shares at any time. Businessmen later created new associations without neighborhood sponsorship.

The new cooperative associations became known as "building and loan" or "savings and loan" associations. They lent money only for residential real estate. Associations provided safe deposit places for savings, and mortgage loans for the immediate neighborhood.

Early Problems

By 1893 there were more than 5,800 savings associations with approximately 1.75 million saver shareholders and over 450,000 borrowers. Government did little to regulate the industry. In 1875 the State of New York implemented the first steps toward regulation by requesting copies of association annual reports on financial conditions. By 1900 the regulation that did exist was minimal, and included only a few states.

As the thrift industry continued to transform itself from small parochial associations into substantial corporations, the increasing demand for mortgage funding provided regional conflicts. In some areas, home loan demand exceeded local depositors' available funds. In other places, the opposite was true. A central credit facility was necessary to receive deposits from cash-heavy thrifts and lend funds to thrifts with high mortgage demand. A few states such as New York attempted to solve this problem by establishing statewide thrift credit facilities. These institutions sold bonds to the capital markets. The bonds were secured by mortgages from member thrift institutions.

The need for a national thrift credit clearinghouse continued to grow. The boom of new housing after World War I far exceeded the available supply of mortgage funds in most areas of the country. The ensuing prosperity of the 1920s effectively masked the underlying thrift problems. Homes were typically financed with one year balloon payment mortgages. The constant rollover of short-term, unamortized loans created continuous refinancing problems. Many borrowers were forced into expensive and risky second liens. As the value of property increased so did the demand for homes and mortgages. Despite these problems, most Americans felt mortgage money was secure and plentiful.

The savings and loan industry had grown to become a major player in American finance. The building boom of the roaring 1920s caused unprecedented growth. By 1928 there were over 12,000 building and loan associations, and more applications in process. Despite this growth, the industry was governed by a patchwork of state and local regulations. Savings institutions had to rely on commercial banks, their main competitors, for funds to supplement savings deposits. Commercial bank funds, meanwhile, were supplied by the Federal Reserve System, which was established by Congress in 1913.

The banks were more organized under the federal system of national banks. The system was federally regulated by the Comptroller of the Currency which promoted safety and soundness through consistent regulations. The industry's orderliness helped banks to publicly oppose any attempted strengthening of state-chartered financial institutions. Proposals to create a Federal Bank System for thrifts were successfully opposed by the commercial banking industry in 1919, 1920, and 1927. Each time, the proposal died because of the banking industry's political power.

The Crash of 1929
The stock market crash and the resulting depression of the early 1930s clearly revealed the deficiencies of the building and loan system. The Great Depression forced over 1,700 thrifts to fail. Depositors lost over $250 million and hysteria prevailed. Because savings accounts were not insured, depositors quickly withdrew their funds at the first rumor of an association's financial problems. Even healthy thrifts were unable to meet the excessive demand for withdrawals. Consequently, depositors' accounts were frozen in place. Black markets developed to purchase passbooks from customers desperate for cash.

As the depression deepened and the unemployment rate hurled upward, defaults on mortgage notes surged. Housing used as collateral for loans declined in value, often falling below the loan amount. Thrifts were forced to repossess property despite the extreme cost to maintain the foreclosed assets. Mortgage foreclosures increased nationally from 70,000 in 1928 to over 285,000 in 1932.

Federal Home Loan Bank Act of 1932

The Depression made it painfully clear that the thrift industry was failing. A reserve bank system for thrifts was urgently needed to act as a central credit facility. On July 16th, under the direction of President Hoover, Congress passed the Federal Home Loan Bank Act of 1932. The Act's primary purpose was to rescue the failing savings and loan industry. Patterned after the Federal Reserve System, the Act created the Federal Home Loan Bank System. The Bank Board would serve as a regulatory agency. Eight to twelve District Banks would become a reserve credit system for member savings and loan associations, mutual savings banks, and insurance companies. This Act also authorized the District Banks to raise funds from the sale of bonds.

The Federal Home Loan Bank Board established 12 District Banks. District lines were based upon current mortgage owners' locations and the need to transfer funds from capital-surplus to capital-poor areas. Therefore, some bank districts comprised much larger areas than others. Bank sizes and the amount of business transacted varied widely. Each Bank carried the name of the city in which it was located.

The Bank Board then selected directors for the 12 Banks. By October 1932, with a staff of 132 people, the Banks were officially chartered and opened for business.

The first goal of the District Banks was the sponsorship of national legislation authorizing home financing institutions to become members of the Bank System. By March 22, 1933, all but five states had passed such enabling legislation.

The District Banks began operations capitalized with $125 million from the United States Treasury. Under the Act, this government money was to be repaid by the Banks once stock purchased by member institutions equalled the amount paid in by the government. By 1951 all the funds supplied by the government had been repaid, and the Banks were wholly owned by their member institutions.

Home Owners' Loan Act of 1933

In 1933, 40 percent of the country's $20 billion in home mortgage loans were in default. Approximately 26,000 loans were being foreclosed each month. In the midst of this crisis, Congress passed and President Roosevelt signed into law on June 13th, the Home Owners' Loan Act of 1933 (HOLA). The HOLA made two significant additions to the original Federal Home Loan Bank Act. First, it created a system of federal savings and loan associations. Second, as an emergency relief it created the Home Owners' Loan Corporation. This entity allowed lending institutions to exchange delinquent mortgages for Home Owners' Loan Corporation bonds. The Bank Board was given substantial regulatory and supervisory powers over federal savings and loans as well as quasi-judicial powers in approving requests for charters, mergers, and branch offices. The federal savings and loan system established local thrift and home financing institutions in areas where they were needed but did not exist. The HOLA also helped ensure the soundness of the entire savings and loan industry by introducing more extensive federal regulation.

The Home Owners' Loan Corporation was designed to strengthen lenders in the home mortgage market. It provided less stringent terms to existing borrowers who were in default on their mortgages. Lenders exchanged delinquent mortgages for bonds of the Home Owners' Loan Corporation. The Corporation then refinanced the mortgage loans for the borrowers on more liberal terms. In this way, the borrowers' obligations were held directly by the Federal government. Savings and loans initially transferred 13 percent of their total mortgage loan portfolio to the Corporation. The $770 million in Home Owners' Loan Corporation bonds that the institutions received in exchange for the mortgage loans alleviated much of the savings and loan associations' financial difficulties. In three years of lending, from June 1933 to June 1936, the Home Owners' Loan Corporation refinanced $2.75 billion worth of home mortgages. Ultimately, it processed over 1.8 million loans amounting to $6.2 billion. The legislation creating the Home Owners' Loan Corporation also provided for its automatic liquidation. Although it had used some government subsidies, the Corporation returned a small profit to the Treasury. In its final years, the Corporation auctioned its remaining mortgage loans in large blocks to savings and loans and other lenders. The Home Owners Loan Corporation legally expired in 1954.

National Housing Act of 1934—The Birth of the FSLIC

Congress enacted the National Housing Act of 1934 to remedy the escalating problems facing the savings and loan industry and to ensure its future stability. The Act established the Federal Savings and Loan Insurance Corporation (FSLIC). The FSLIC was established to extend deposit insurance to savings institutions, as the Federal Deposit Insurance Corporation (FDIC) provided deposit insurance for commercial banks. Both insurance corporations began operating in 1934, and insurance coverage has been parallel since then. The limit on insurance, originally $5,000 for each saver in each institution, rose steadily to $10,000 in 1950, $15,000 in 1966, $20,000 in 1969, $40,000 in 1974, and $100,000 in 1980.

Despite its obvious benefits, state-chartered thrifts were slow to accept FSLIC insurance because it subjected them to federal regulation, examination, and supervision. Many state-chartered thrifts also chafed at paying the deposit insurance premiums. By mid-1936 only 30 percent or 1,336 thrifts were FSLIC-insured. All but 237 of these were federally chartered thrifts which were required by law to carry the insurance. It took until 1951 for FSLIC-insured institutions to outnumber non-FSLIC-insured institutions. By then, insured thrifts held more than 90 percent of all the assets in the savings and loan industry. By the end of 1985, the FSLIC insured 92.6 percent or 2,960 savings and loan associations which held 98.5 percent of the assets of the savings and loan industry.

As part of its role in insuring accounts, the FSLIC worked to stabilize insured thrifts that were wavering on failure. If possible, the FSLIC provided loans to the troubled institution, arranged for it to be taken over by a stronger institution, or took other steps to prevent default. Only if the institution was beyond help did the FSLIC take it over and pay out its insured deposits to savers.

By 1939 the nation's economy was recovering. The Bank Board had existed for seven years. During that time, the Bank System had rescued the thrift industry from potential collapse and shepherded federally chartered thrifts into existence across the U.S. The FHLBB established the FSLIC insurance program. Through the HOLC, the Board enabled over one million Americans to retain their homes despite crippling economic conditions.

Home Owners' Loan Act of 1935

Under the Home Owners' Loan Act of 1935, the Federal Savings and Loan Advisory Council was established. This independent advisory body is empowered to advise the Federal Home Loan Bank Board on general business conditions and special matters affecting the Federal Home Loan Banks, their members, and the FSLIC. The Council is authorized to request information and make recommendations with regard to matters within the Bank Board's jurisdiction. The Council consists of 24 members. The board of directors of each Bank elects one member per annum, and the Board annually appoints the remaining members. The council meets twice a year at the Board's offices in Washington, D.C.

The War Years, 1939-1947

Although by 1939 the Federal Savings and Loan System had grown significantly, it had not matured to the point where it constituted a major political force. The Board had not existed long enough to establish itself firmly as an independent agency. There was conflict as a result of the savings and loan industry's lack of support of the President's public housing efforts. Under President Roosevelt's Reorganization Plan No. 1, which Congress approved in 1939, the Bank Board was consolidated with other agencies into the newly formed Federal Loan Agency.

The next organizational change came in 1942 when the Bank Board was transferred to the National Housing Agency. The National Housing Agency amalgamated sixteen different housing-related agencies that were grouped into three major subunits: the Federal Home Loan Bank Administration, the Federal Public Housing Authority, and the Federal Housing Administration. The Federal Home Loan Bank Administration included all the subunits that were previously under the Board's jurisdiction: the FSLIC, the HOLC, the FHLBank System, and the Federal Savings and Loan System. The Federal Home Loan Bank Administration was given the responsibility of liquidating the U.S. Housing Corporation which was completed in 1945. The U.S. Housing Corporation had been set up in 1918 for the purpose of providing housing for workers in congested war production centers.

The Federal Home Loan Bank Administration actively continued the work of the HOLC from 1939 to 1947. Because the economy showed major improvement, the HOLC's effort proceeded rapidly. Lower interest rates and monthly payments enabled borrowers to pay off their debts, thus significantly reducing the number of foreclosures. The other main concern of the Bank Administration during this period was that the heated wartime economy would lead savings and loans to make many of the same mistakes that led to the problems of the Depression. This fear was evident in supervisory policies.

Another major effort of the Bank Administration was to facilitate the consolidation of the savings and loan industry. From 1939 to 1940 over 1,900 thrift institutions were in a gradual state of liquidation. These associations did not make new loans and received no new share investments. Operations were restricted to the collection of mortgage loan interest and principal and to the sale of real estate owned. These small non-FSLIC-insured associations were merged out of existence by liquidating the assets.

During this period, the flow of savings into savings and loans increased steadily. Indeed, some savings and loans even wanted to restrict deposits because private housing was not being built in the private sector. As a result of the housing shortage, thrifts were able to sell most of the foreclosed real estate acquired during the

Depression years. The Federal Home Loan Bank Administration remained part of the National Housing Agency until July 1947, when it became part of the newly created Housing and Home Finance Agency.

Growth and Prosperity, 1948-1960

The 1950s were a period of dramatic growth and prosperity for the savings and loan industry. The total assets of the industry grew from $10 billion in 1947 to over $60 billion in 1959. California, Ohio, and New York were the fastest growing areas.

With the exception of relatively moderate credit shortages followed by mild recessions in 1950, 1954, and 1955, the economy was generally very strong. Interests rates for savings were 2 to 2.5 percent and home mortgage notes were 5 to 5.5 percent. Rates were usually low and stable; however, by 1959 the savings rate was 4 percent and trending upward. In that same year, the first instance of disintermediation (a major shift of funds to higher yielding investments) was experienced. The Treasury issued a four year, ten month certificate at 5 percent, reflecting the increased competition for savings. Demand for residential mortgages remained strong with little competition from commercial banks. During this time frame, national financial transactions and thrift usage of the secondary mortgage markets became more common.

The Bank Board regained its independent status with the Housing Act of 1955, which removed the Bank Board from the Housing and Home Finance Agency. This separation came mainly as a result of the persistent efforts of the industry's trade associations. The action had been recommended earlier that year by the Commission on the Organization of the Executive Branch of Government, also known as the "Hoover Commission."

The Bank Board's priorities shifted significantly during this time. The HOLC, which was the predominant concern of the Board from 1933 to 1947, was rapidly winding down. The Board's new top priority was the support and regulation of the rapidly expanding industry.

The Bank Board began taking a more active role in the lending function of the District Banks. This was necessitated by the minor credit crunch in 1950, precipitated by the Korean War, and by more severe credit shortages in 1955 and 1959. One of the Board's main concerns was to coordinate the policies of the District Banks with the economic policies of the Federal government.

The Board's regulatory authority gradually increased. In 1950 the Bank Board allowed federal savings and loans to adopt new charters. This gave savings and loan management much greater leeway in structuring savings accounts. However, in return, the Board obtained more authority over the associations. Also in 1950, the Federal Home Loan Bank Act was amended authorizing the Board to impose liquidity requirements on each Federal Home Loan Bank member.

Requests to open branch locations generated an increased workload for the Bank Board. Between 1952 and 1959, over 830 branch applications were reviewed by the Board. Approving these applications was a time consuming effort as many required public hearings. In response to the increased workload, the Board's staff steadily expanded. By 1959 there were 952 total employees, and 674 were examiners.

A Rapidly Changing World, 1961-1970

During the 1960s, thrift industry assets grew in excess of $80 billion. However, the thrift industry foundation, which was based on stable interest rates and nominal competition, was slowly beginning to crumble. Increased competition from commercial banks, rising interest rates, and higher taxes negatively affected the thrifts. These changes caused industry earnings to decline. The rise in the cost of funds to savings associations supplemented the thrifts' inability to alter their portfolio structures.

The other, more dramatic symptom of the underlying problems of the savings and loan industry was the first severe disintermediation period that came in 1966. This reoccurred in 1969 and early 1970 when, for the first time after World War II, there was a net outflow of savings. During these periods, due to rate controls, savings flowed from savings and loans and commercial banks to higher yielding investments. The U.S. was undergoing a series of credit crunches. These occurred because the Federal government did not raise taxes to fund the Vietnam War, the new social programs, and the increased business expansion. Moreover, the Federal Reserve was reluctant to expand the money supply to ease the credit shortage fearing that the inflation rate would also increase.

To ensure thrift industry stability, Congress strengthened the regulator's authority to impose interest rate ceilings on member association savings accounts. This was done with the Interest Rate Control Act of 1966. In addition, the Federal Reserve received increased authority to regulate rates on commercial bank deposits. Congress wanted thrifts to pay slightly higher rates on deposits than commercial banks. Congress also set up a committee consisting of the heads of the financial regulatory agencies to coordinate their rate control efforts.

Until the late 1950s, if a savings and loan was conducting unsafe or unsound practices, the Bank Board generally dealt with the situation on a case-by-case basis. Starting in the early 1960s, however, the Board changed this approach. It adopted a sizable number of regulations that applied uniformly to all federally insured savings and loans. Despite the efforts of the Board, there was a growing awareness that the problems of the industry were not being addressed effectively.

The Onslaught of Regulation, 1971-1982

Throughout the 1970s, thrifts faced increasing legislative activity. The Housing and Community Development Act of 1974 liberalized lending powers for federally chartered associations. The Real Estate Settlement Procedures Act of 1974, as amended in 1976, required lenders to inform loan customers in advance of the total estimated charges to be assessed in granting mortgages. The Equal Credit Opportunity Act of 1974 prohibited discrimination in credit transactions on the basis of sex, marital status, race, color, religion, national origin, receipt of public assistance benefits, or the borrower's good faith exercise of rights under the Consumer Credit Protection Act.

The Home Mortgage Disclosure Act of 1975 required most depository institutions to disclose to the public the number and dollar amount of mortgage loans originated or purchased in each census tract. The Community Reinvestment Act of 1977 required federal regulatory agencies to encourage financial institutions to accommodate all community credit needs, including low and moderate income neighborhoods. The Financial Institutions Regulatory and Interest Rate Control Act of 1978 authorized the FSLIC to contribute financial assistance while arranging the merger or acquisition of a failed institution by a strong institution. Financial assistance was an important new tool in dealing with insolvent thrifts.

The Depository Institutions Deregulation and Monetary Control Act of 1980 mandated the gradual removal by 1986 of all interest rate controls on federally regulated depository institutions. Authority to implement the phase-out was assigned to a new umbrella group called the Depository Institutions Deregulation Committee (DIDC). This panel was composed of the Secretary of the Treasury and the heads of the federal financial regulatory agencies.

Prior to the DIDC activity, the Bank Board had already begun using its regulatory authority to banish interest rate restraints. In 1978 the Bank Board permitted savings and loans to offer money market certificates with interest rates tied to Treasury bill rates. In 1980 the Bank Board authorized the 30 month Small Savers' Certificates. The new savings instruments proved an expensive way to attract savings because thrift options for investing funds remained tightly regulated. To counter the higher cost of funds, the Bank Board authorized federally chartered associations to offer variable rate mortgages in 1979. These debt instruments allowed mortgage rate spreads to keep pace with interest rates paid on savings accounts.

Trial by Interest Rates

Market interest rates were both exceptionally high and extremely volatile in 1979 and 1980. By the end of 1980, many thrifts were in deep trouble, with a severe negative mismatch between the yields on assets and the costs of liabilities. Most of the industry's interest-bearing assets were in long-term home mortgages with low, fixed-rates of interest. More than half of its interest-bearing liabilities were in short-term (one year or less) certificates of deposit (CDs) paying high, deregulated market rates. By 1981 associations paid an average cost of funds rate of 11.53 percent while earning an average mortgage portfolio return of only 10.02 percent.

But thrifts had little choice. They had to pay high rates to savers to avoid losing their deposits to the money market funds, which had no regulatory limit on earnings. Even so, during 1981 and 1982, savers withdrew $31.8 billion more than they deposited in FSLIC-insured thrifts.

In the face of its negative yield and heavy deposit outflows, the thrift industry experienced staggering losses. Red ink totaled $8.9 billion in 1981 and 1982, with a record $3.3 billion loss in the first half of 1982, and a $6 billion decline in net worth. In the last six months of 1981, 85 percent of all associations insured by the FSLIC operated at a loss.

From 1981 to 1982, 813 saving institutions disappeared; most of them merged into other institutions. The Bank Board arranged 342 of those mergers. To forestall liquidation, 92 thrifts received financial assistance from the FSLIC while two other associations were liquidated. So intense was the search for healthy merger partners that in September 1981, the Bank Board allowed the FSLIC to arrange interstate mergers, breaking the long-held ban on branching across state lines.

Although the industry's troubles were common knowledge, FSLIC deposit insurance prevented the public panic associated with the Depression of the 1930s. Long lines of desperate people did not form to withdraw savings. The public's faith was maintained by the federal deposit insurance program.

Chapter 2.

THE 1980's: CRISIS MANAGEMENT

The Garn-St Germain
Depository Institutions Act of 1982

The thrift industry crisis evoked the most significant thrift legislation in half a century. The Garn-St Germain Depository Institutions Act of 1982 was signed into law by President Ronald Reagan on October 15, 1982. Garn-St Germain contained three landmark provisions giving thrifts new business opportunities to help them survive financial storms. The legislation granted the Bank Board and the FSLIC new powers to deal with financially troubled associations. It authorized an emergency rescue program to assist savings institutions that were troubled, but basically sound.

Garn-St Germain differed fundamentally from the reforms of the 1930s in that it deregulated rather than regulated. The legislation balanced the potential return on assets to the cost of funds. The Act gave the industry flexibility to respond to rapidly changing market conditions. The legislation mandated the phase-out of existing interest rate differentials by January 1984, and introduced two other main deregulatory aspects. First, it allowed the DIDC to authorize thrifts and banks to issue money market deposit accounts. Bearing no interest limit, these accounts could compete directly with money market mutual funds. Second, the Act gave savings institutions limited authority to expand into areas such as commercial lending, traditionally reserved for banks.

The money market deposit account was introduced in December 1982. During its first four months, it proved an enormous success by attracting more than $108 billion in savings to FSLIC-insured institutions. For the first time in nearly two years, savers were depositing more funds in thrifts than they were withdrawing.

The new asset powers also proved beneficial. The new business opportunities allowed thrifts to bolster financial strength while completing their primary mission of financing home ownership. Garn-St Germain allowed thrifts to increase short-term assets, which could be adjusted quickly to changing interest rates. In particular, the Act gave all federal associations the power to:

- Make commercial, corporate, business, or agricultural loans, which after January 1, 1984, could constitute up to 10 percent of an association's assets.

- Increase from 20 percent to 30 percent the amount of assets available for consumer loans, and make inventory and floor planning loans beyond existing authority.

- Offer individual or corporate demand deposit accounts. Corporate checking accounts could be opened only by companies having other business with the association.

- Increase from 20 percent to 40 percent the amount of assets that could be invested in loans secured by nonresidential real estate.

- Invest up to 10 percent of assets in personal property for rent or sale.

- Make education loans for any educational purpose, instead of just for college or vocational training.

- Invest up to 100 percent of assets in state or local government obligations.

- Invest in other thrifts' time deposits and savings deposits and use the investments to help meet liquidity requirements.

Garn-St Germain realigned the industry's structure by eliminating differences in the kinds of business in which federal savings and loan associations and federal savings banks were allowed to engage. The Act made it easier for savings and loan associations to become savings banks and vice versa. It allowed existing institutions to select either the stock or the mutual form of ownership.

Before Garn-St Germain was enacted, all new federally chartered savings and loan associations had to begin operation as mutual companies. Mutual institutions are mutually owned by all of a thrift's depositors and borrowers. Traditionally, a saver was entitled to one vote for every $100 or fraction thereof of savings, and each borrower was entitled to one vote. Throughout most of the thrift industry's history, savers were called shareholders rather than depositors. Every time savers put money into a thrift, they technically bought shares in an association. Most savers signed proxies authorizing the institution's management to exercise their voting rights associated with the shares. Mutual thrift institutions declared dividends on the shares. To savers, these earnings looked just like interest, but legally they were dividends.

In contrast to the mutual thrift institutions, stock savings and loan associations belong to persons who buy stock in the corporation. These stockholders may or may not be depositors or borrowers. Ownership of stock is not a condition for conducting business with the thrift. Garn-St Germain permitted newly formed thrift institutions to receive federal charters and organize as stock corporations. The 1982 legislation also made it easier for existing federally chartered mutual thrifts to convert to stock ownership upon FSLIC approval.

Garn-St Germain ended an advantage thrifts had enjoyed for nearly two decades: the privilege of paying savers a slightly higher interest rate than commercial banks. The Act imposed on thrifts the same anti-tying prohibitions that applied to commercial banks. This move prevented associations from requiring applicants for one type of service, such as a loan, to use other services as a condition for receiving the original service.

Beyond giving thrifts new business opportunities, Garn-St Germain expanded federal regulators' powers to deal with financially troubled institutions. Perhaps most important, the legislation granted the Bank Board the power to override state authorities to appoint the FSLIC as Receiver of bankrupt state-chartered FSLIC-insured thrifts. Garn-St Germain also reaffirmed FSLIC and Bank Board authority to cross state lines to merge a failed institution with another insured institution. The Act gave the FSLIC new authority to keep thrifts solvent by depositing money in them or buying their securities.

Finally, Garn-St Germain authorized a new capital assistance program for troubled thrift institutions. This program was called the Net Worth Certificate Program. Qualifying associations with less than a 3 percent net worth were permitted to secure promissory notes from the FSLIC in exchange for instruments, issued by thrifts, called net worth certificates. Because the FSLIC's promissory notes guaranteed the notes' face amounts, thrifts could use them to raise their net worth to the required minimum, and thereby hold off an FSLIC takeover. As institutions regained financial health, they would begin trading back the promissory notes for the net worth certificates. If all went well, the obligations eventually would be canceled, with no cash ever changing hands.

The Decline in Interest Rates

As dramatic and far-reaching as Garn-St Germain was, the Act alone could not have saved the thrift industry. Although thrift institutions were experts in home financing, they needed time to master other types of loans. The Act by itself could not grant them the time.

During the second half of 1982, interest rates began declining, and by year-end associations were again earning more interest than they were paying. During the first six months of 1983, the industry's overall cost of funds was 9.81 percent, while the average portfolio yield was 11.04 percent.

Nonetheless, 35 percent of all the FSLIC-insured thrift institutions were still losing money by the end of 1983. Their financial conditions were unsalvageable. The ratio of regulatory net worth to total assets was less than 3 percent at more than one fourth of all the FSLIC-insured institutions. The industry's earnings and net worth figures would have been even lower without certain temporary accounting techniques the Bank Board permitted thrifts to use.

During 1984 the thrift industry continued to grow rapidly. Deposits in FSLIC-insured institutions increased by 17 percent to $784.7 billion and assets grew by 19 percent to $978.5 billion. By contrast, the FSLIC's reserves declined 12.7 percent to $5.6 billion and at the end of 1984 the ratio of the FSLIC reserves to insured savings deposits had dropped to 0.78 percent.

In 1985, restricted by new Bank Board regulations, the pace of deposit growth slowed sharply to about half that of 1984. Liability growth, which had risen by 19.4 percent from 1983 to 1984, was down to 7.5 percent above the 1984 figure. But the FSLIC's reserves dropped further to $4.6 billion and the reserve ratio fell to 0.55 percent.

Increased Thrift Failures

The FSLIC's difficulties stemmed from the continuing high levels of thrift failures. But whereas the failures during 1981 and 1982 resulted primarily from high interest rates, the failures in 1984 and 1985 resulted from defaulting loans and investments. The FSLIC resolved 35 cases during 1985; 26 of the institutions failed because of problems related to asset quality. These problems were expensive to resolve and substantially decreased the FSLIC's reserves. In 1984 and 1985, 19 institutions were placed in FSLIC receivership for liquidation.

Additional Regulations

To reduce the FSLIC's risk of exposure, the Bank Board took steps to curb risk taking by insured institutions and provide closer monitoring of thrift activities. In January 1985 the Board adopted regulations that linked net worth requirements to growth rates. The regulations required thrifts to obtain supervisory approval before undertaking potentially risky ventures. Approval was compulsory before investing more than 10 percent of a thrift's assets in equity securities, real estate, or subsidiary service corporations.

Regulators found increased examination and supervision necessary because thrifts' freedom of choice in investing had grown. To strengthen the examination of institutions, the Bank Board in July 1985 delegated the responsibility for conducting examinations to the District Banks. The Board's examiners and support staff were transferred to the employ of the District Banks. The move placed the examiners under the same roofs as the District Banks' supervisory agents. The supervisory agents enforced corrective measures at thrift institutions upon the examiners' discovery of violations. The transfer provided faster response to early warning signals of institutions' financial problems.

As 1984 came to a close, the net worth of the Bank System's member institutions received a boost in the form of 15 million shares (with a market value of about $600 million) of participating, preferred, nonvoting stock in the Federal Home Loan Mortgage Corporation. Freddie Mac distributed the stock as a special dividend and dictated that nearly all future dividends would go directly to member thrift institutions, rather than to the District Banks, which hold Freddie Mac's common stock. By including the dividend, FSLIC-insured thrift institutions posted 1984 earnings of $1.1 billion, representing a return on assets of 0.12 percent.

In 1985, market interest rates fell, and most institutions reduced interest rate risk and improved profitability. FSLIC-insured associations achieved the highest aggregate return on assets since 1979, earning net income three and one half times that of 1984. Gross mortgage lending was up. The market value of the thrift industry's residential mortgage holdings exceeded book value for the first time since 1979.

However, 15 percent of the industry continued to experience operating losses. Serious problems were encountered because of unsound lending and investment practices. More than one fifth of the industry had a regulatory net worth ratio below 3 percent.

The Management Consignment Program

Early in 1985 the Federal Home Loan Bank Board, the FSLIC, and the District Banks jointly agreed that the FSLIC did not possess sufficient resources to deal with the significant number of emerging troubled thrifts throughout the United States. From this general consensus evolved a proposed solution called the Management Consignment Program (MCP). Through this program under authority derived from the National Housing Act, healthy, well-managed thrifts would be employed by the District Banks on a short-term basis to provide management expertise to insolvent associations. The intent was to provide expert management skills to protect the failing thrifts' assets. The FSLIC would benefit by the reduction of risk and loss until final resolution of the problem. Specific program goals included the stabilization of the deposit base, thus eliminating high interest rate solicitations, control of problem assets, and the positioning of the institution for eventual sale by the FSLIC.

The first MCP was created in California on April 23, 1985, when Beverly Hills (CA) Savings and Loan Association was placed into FSLIC Receivership. First Nationwide Savings of San Francisco was contracted by the FSLIC to assume the management of the assets and liabilities that were transferred into a new (de novo) federal association. While the MCP was initially established as a stabilization and evaluation technique for only the short term, the funding problems of the FSLIC have resulted in a long-term operation. Through the end of 1986, 45 savings and loans had been funded into the program and by year end 1987 over 62 were included.

The program developed into four classifications. Type I involved a voluntary MCP in which directors were replaced and new management installed. FSLIC indemnification was given to the new management and stock ownership continued. Type II included the FHLBB appointment of a Conservator, while existing directors were replaced by an advisory board. The Conservator hired an institution to provide daily management. Type III encompassed the actual closing of the thrift institution. The FSLIC was appointed receiver and transferred all the assets and liabilities to a new federal mutual association chartered by the FHLBB. The new institution then employed another thrift to manage the assets and liabilities. Stockholder rights and claims were eliminated, yet all insured and uninsured accounts were passed through to the new association. This situation was known as a Pass-Through Receivership. Type IV entailed the FSLIC as receiver transferring insured deposits and performing assets to a newly created federal institution. The FSLIC liquidated the bad assets. Stockholders interests were wiped out and uninsured accounts were not transferred to the new association. This kind of transaction was known as an asset-backed transfer of accounts.

The problem with the MCP thrifts involved their enormous costs. Each institution that remained open for business drained the thrift industry and the FSLIC with millions of dollars of monthly losses. The American taxpayer ultimately paid because he funded both the savings industry and the FSLIC. Since 1985 over $3 billion was spent on MCP operations, with a negative worth cumulatively exceeding $5.5 billion.

Reasons for the dire performance of MCP thrifts ranged from the FSLIC's scarcity of funding to lack of incentives for the new MCP managers. In many cases, the original institution was so poorly managed that loan documentation and general business records were nonexistent. Extremely complex and cumbersome loan participations, often with other insolvent savings and loan participants, demanded intense negotiation because of the lack of written binding agreements. MCP managers were not trained or equipped to handle these conditions. While the expertise of these managers was lending money and operating profitable thrifts, they were often faced with tedious workout negotiations and mounting litigation. Furthermore, questions were raised by industry executives concerning conflicts of interest. This caused the hesitancy of some healthy thrifts to participate. Close relations with parent thrift operations made it difficult for MCP managers to exhibit competitive partiality. Some problems of insolvent thrifts were simply beyond the control of any manager including the FSLIC. Ultimately, the FSLIC had to discontinue the MCP program.

Competitive Equality Banking Act of 1987 (CEBA)

The enactment of the Competitive Equality Banking Act of 1987 (CEBA) reflected the determination of the 100th Congress to mend the U.S. financial system and restore confidence in financial institutions. The Competitive Equality Banking Act of 1987 was a product of legislative and executive branch compromises and protracted debates. The CEBA was designed to alleviate the problems that led to the largest number of bank and savings and loan association failures since the Great Depression. It addressed six major provisions. The law regulated nonbank banks; imposed a moratorium on certain securities, insurance, and real estate activities by banks; recapitalized the Federal Savings and Loan Insurance Corporation; allowed emergency interstate bank acquisitions; streamlined credit union operations; and regulated consumer check holds.

Depository Institutions Failures

The Competitive Equality Banking Act of 1987 permanently renewed the expired provisions from the Garn-St Germain Act which have let regulators find emergency acquisitions for closed failed banks and thrifts. In addition, it extended for five years the Garn-St Germain program authorizing the issuance of net worth certificates to bolster thrift capital.

Nonbank Banks

The CEBA closed the so-called nonbank bank loophole in the Bank Holding Company Act by redefining the definition of the term "bank." Nonbank banks established prior to March 5, 1987, could continue to operate, but restrictions were imposed on their growth.

Nonbank banks were an innovative corporate form developed in the marketplace to avoid certain restrictive banking laws. Their use allowed both banking and nonbanking firms to expand their banking operations in ways that otherwise would not have been possible.

Specifically, nonbank banks were institutions which limited their activities to avoid being defined as banks under the Bank Holding Company Act, the federal law governing bank holding companies. Parent companies were not subject to the law's ownership and geographic restrictions. Nonetheless, the bank itself was chartered by either a federal or state authority and was subject to regulations of its regulatory agencies.

Glass-Steagall Extension

The CEBA extended until March 1, 1988, the Glass-Steagall prohibitions on the mixing of banking and commerce to depository institutions that were not members of the Federal Reserve. State-chartered, non-Federal Reserve member banks and subsidiaries of FSLIC-insured savings and loans were prevented from affiliating with securities firms during this moratorium. Section 20 of Glass-Steagall prohibited a member bank from affiliating with a company that was principally engaged in underwriting of securities. Section 32 of Glass-Steagall prohibited interlocking directorates between member banks and persons engaged primarily in the securities business. Federal regulators were prohibited from permitting banks to engage in new real estate, insurance, and securities activities during the moratorium period.

Interstate Banking

Prior to the CEBA, an out-of-state holding company which acquired a bank or bank holding company under the emergency provisions could acquire additional banks. They could establish branches in-state within two years of the acquisition, or earlier if permitted under state law. The CEBA required the FDIC to consider the adverse economic impact that the liquidation of loans from closed banks had on a local community, and publish procedures to minimize the consequences. Moreover, the CEBA directed the FDIC to work with state-authorized capital pools to save community banks. The CEBA encouraged loan sales to area banks to prevent further asset devaluation in a given area.

Funds Availability

The CEBA required depository institutions to make funds available to depositors for checks written on local banks after two intervening business days, starting in September 1988; and after one intervening business day, starting in 1990. Depository institutions were permitted to hold funds for checks written on out-of-town banks for a maximum of six intervening business days starting September 1988, and four intervening business days in 1990. The CEBA placed limits on the number of days a depository institution could restrict the availability of funds which are deposited in any account.

Recapitalization of the FSLIC and Forbearance

The CEBA authorized establishment of a special financing corporation funded initially by the Federal Home Loan Banks. The corporation would sell bonds in the capital market to raise funds for the FSLIC. The borrowings would be repaid through investment in zero coupon instruments that would serve as collateral for the borrowed funds. This new financing corporation was authorized to raise $10.8 billion for the FSLIC. FSLIC spending from this fund was limited to no more than $3.75 billion a year to close down insolvent thrifts.

Supervisory forbearance was required by the CEBA. It obligated the Federal Home Loan Bank Board to give well managed but troubled thrifts in the energy and agricultural belts time to work out their problems. Thrifts in the oil and farm regions with net worth as low as 0.5 percent could be granted forbearance if the Bank Board determined that the individual institution had a chance of recovery. Farm banks were permitted to write down farm loans over a seven year period, rather than immediately reducing loan losses from capital.

The FHLBB Implements the CEBA

The Competitive Equality Banking Act was signed into federal law by President Ronald Reagan on August 10, 1987. Because the legislation provided the recapitalization of the FSLIC Insurance Fund, political maneuvering played a major role in the law's final form. Congressional committees negotiated for months to finalize a recapitalization of the bankrupt insurance system, eventually agreeing to $10.8 billion. A wide array of financial issues allowed Congress to make sweeping changes in bank and thrift institution oversight. The Bank Board was directed to narrow the gap between existing thrift oversight and the proven federal banking regulations.

The Bank Board immediately began implementation of the bill's required changes upon passage of the Act. Congress even set a deadline for the new FHLBB rules to be implemented. By January 5, 1988, the abstract ideas mandated by Congress had to be transformed into federal regulations. That meant proposing the new regulations and considering comments voiced at public hearings. Regulatory staffs had to be trained to effectively administer the changes. A thrift institution training package had to be developed. The following is a brief summary of the new Bank Board regulations adopted for the CEBA.

The Bank Board established a definite timetable for savings and loan institutions to convert from Regulatory Accounting Practices (RAP) to Generally Accepted Accounting Principles (GAAP).

Section 402 of the CEBA required new thrift appraisal standards that would be consistent with those utilized by the federal banking agencies. Effective January 7, 1988, R-41C, the Bank Board's appraisal guideline memorandum, was rescinded. The new rule shifted responsibility for implementation of appraisal policy to each insured thrift's management.

Thrift institutions were mandated to adopt an asset classification system similar to federal banking agencies. Revised regulations expanded the classification of all assets. Existing classification categories of Substandard, Doubtful, and Loss were retained and a Special Mention rating was added.

The establishment of individual minimum capital requirements and capital directives allowed the Bank Board to use its discretion when evaluating savings institutions for sound financial practices.

A capital forbearance regulation established a mechanism for regulatory forbearance for well managed FSLIC-insured institutions. The regulation clarified qualifying criteria while extending the Bank Board's 1987 Capital Forbearance Policy Statement.

A qualified thrift lender test was designed to answer Congressional concern that the thrift industry was not emphasizing housing needs. The test required at least 60 percent of each thrift's total tangible assets to be qualifying thrift investments. These investments included loans, securities or equities in residential real estate, business property, and other liquid assets.

Application processing guidelines were implemented by the Bank Board to eliminate Congressional concerns that the Bank System was not responding in a timely manner to applications filed by institutions. The time limits applied to the Bank Board and the Federal Home Loan District Banks.

Troubled Debt Restructuring (TDR) procedures already being used by thrifts were formalized by the universal application of financial statement standards and net realizable value analyses.

What is the FICO?

The most strategic aspect of the CEBA was the creation of the Financing Corporation (FICO). The FICO was authorized to sell up to $10.8 billion in bonds over three years. Principal on the bonds is secured by zero-coupon Treasury notes. The interest is financed by regular and special insurance premiums paid by thrifts. An annual cap of $3.75 billion worth of bond issuances for case resolutions was also instituted.

The FICO is a separate corporation operating under the direction of the Bank Board. The 12 Federal Home Loan Banks will contribute as much as $3 billion in retained earnings. The separate corporation structure is necessary to insulate the District Banks from any reduction in their superior capital market standing. Each of the Federal Home Loan Banks must escrow a set percentage of their retained earnings that cannot be paid out as dividends. Those retained earnings are utilized to purchase stock in the FICO. The Financing Corporation then buys capital stocks in the FSLIC.

After the District Banks purchase the FICO stock with cash, the funds are then leveraged by borrowing in the capital markets. The borrowings are in the form of long-term bonds. The debt is raised gradually as needed. This flexibility enables the FSLIC recapitalization plan to deal with the insurance fund's case resolutions on an "as needed" basis. Congressional oversight ensures careful use of the funds.

The bonds issued by the FICO have maturities of fifteen to thirty years. Such maturities are longer than the typical District Bank offerings. The longer debt maturities are intended to provide the FSLIC with enough time to meet its immediate failed thrift resolution needs, yet return to a healthy state in the longer term future.

The FICO invests long-term debt in FSLIC capital stock. The two capital stock classes issued are redeemable nonvoting and nonredeemable capital certificates. Total insurance fund resources exceeding $25 billion can be realized with the combination of current reserves, FSLIC investment income, future insurance premium contributions, and the new capital stock. The FSLIC pays stock dividends to cover the FICO interest payments to bond holders. Thrift insurance premiums assure the regularity of interest payments. The FICO, not the FSLIC, guarantees principal payments on the bonds.

Acting in a trustee capacity, the FICO invests some retained earnings contributed by the Federal Home Loan Banks in high-quality securities. The goal is to compound sufficient interest to ensure repayment of bond principal over a 20 to 30 year period. Investments such as zero coupon bonds can readily meet this need. Thus, the District Banks' retained earnings provide maximum leverage in the capital markets, yet still retire the outstanding bond principal.

In recent years the speed of thrift industry development overtook statutory guidance, leaving much financial institution regulation to the nation's courts, states, and federal regulators. The CEBA has clarified many of the regulatory concerns in the banking community, particularly regarding nonbank banks, interstate takeover of failing institutions, and foreign banks' domestic operations. Still, there are CEBA provisions that will need revisions in the future: the FSLIC recapitalization and forbearance provisions. Because the initial $10.8 billion funding is inadequate, the mechanism to bail out failed institutions will need further legislation.

The Southwest Plan

Until the 1980's, there was little public concern for savings and loan insolvencies. Between 1972 and 1979 only 21 savings institutions failed. However, in the eight years beginning from 1980 to 1987, 329 thrifts collapsed for an average of over 40 failures per year. Fiscal year 1988 presented even more insolvencies than 1987. These totals were considerably greater than the cumulative total number of failures over the past fifty years. While the number of thrift failures increased, the FSLIC reserve steadily declined. Until the 1980s, insolvencies cost only a minor portion of the annual premium charged by the FSLIC to member thrifts' deposit bases.

Although the thrift industry had experienced a solid track record of earnings before 1980, economic forces such as the Southwest region's oil patch and agricultural downturns created havoc for federal regulators. Some states, notably Texas and California, allowed state-chartered thrift institutions excessive latitude in speculative investments. Despite the high risk, liberal savings and loans still operated with FSLIC deposit insurance. Industry capital requirements, despite sizeable loss experience, were not increased until significant damage had been done. The Bank Board failed for many years to limit direct equity in real estate and other speculative investments. Forbearance demands by Congress to prevent closures and liquidations of failed thrifts magnified past mistakes.

In January 1988 the Federal Home Loan Bank Board was overwhelmed by the tremendous losses of hundreds of insolvent thrifts and the associated Management Consignment Program burden. To counter the growing congressional and industry pressure for action, the Bank Board announced the implementation of the Southwest Plan.

The Plan was revised several times before its formal introduction. House Speaker Jim Wright, D, Texas, demanded assurances that small financial institutions would not be singled out for merging over larger institutions. The concept of statewide megathrifts was also dropped since these creations would also exhibit a competitive advantage over small commercial banks.

The Southwest thrift industry recovery plan contained two major programs. By the end of 1988, the Southwest Plan was designed to merge 104 insolvent Texas savings and loan associations into 39 other weakly capitalized institutions with an estimated FSLIC cost of $7 billion. The program would gradually dissolve the Management Consignment Program in Texas and would result in 22 to 42 consolidated institutions in 14 Texas regions. These new thrifts would include local entities with up to $800 million in assets, regional thrifts with $800 million to $2.5 billion in assets, and interstate associations with more than $2.5 billion in assets.

The FHLBB indicated that the Southwest consolidation plan would provide a mechanism for reducing expenses and controlling losses from troubled thrift assets. The agency projected that expenses would be reduced through a reduction of overlapping and duplicate facilities. In addition, the FHLBB anticipated that losses from troubled assets would be controlled since only the most capable thrift managers would be retained in the consolidation. The FHLBB emphasized that in restructuring the industry, the use of its cash would be minimized. The FSLIC would gain a share in the future profits of the assisted institutions. The FHLBB also expected the plan to attract a substantial inflow of private capital.

In addition to this consolidation plan, the agency attempted to lower the cost of funds at Southwest thrifts by implementing a series of certificate of deposit (CD) programs that would lower the risk premiums on deposits of the most troubled thrifts. The Federal Home Loan Bank of Dallas (FHLB-Dallas) introduced several programs to accomplish this objective. The goal of these funding programs was to market FSLIC-insured CDs in the national money market to reduce the aggressive bidding practices of insolvent thrifts in local market areas. These indirect funding programs did not attract much investor interest. Although the cost of funds declined in some local markets, deposit premiums were not eliminated.

Thrift Industry Perceptions of the Southwest Plan

According to the thrift industry, the primary problem of the savings industry was that there were too many savings and loan institutions. The thrift industry had to be downsized and consolidated to a size that customer markets could support. As an example, in late 1987 there were over 280 savings associations in Texas with more than 1,800 branches. Just as the Texas oil and real estate industries were forced to contract, the thrift industry through government action and natural consolidation would end up with no more than 75 thrifts. All Southwest industries would face the fact that the expected explosive growth into the 1990s simply did not happen. A supply side almost four times as large as potential demand had to be rectified.

The Southwest Plan was the first step back to reality. It was designed to gradually revalue Southwest real estate through federally assisted mergers of failed associations into somewhat healthy associations. Premium rates offered for Texas deposits had to decline to the same interest rates paid by institutions in other states. Before the plan's commencement, Texas thrifts paid between 90 and 120 basis points more for money than Lone Star commercial banks. The final result would be a decrease in the cost of funds nationwide. Excessive and unnecessary overhead would no longer drain the industry. Although not an immediate cure, the Southwest Plan strategy would cushion losses of insolvent associations and precipitate the recovery process.

The FSLIC's goal was to stabilize the thrift industry. As failing thrifts bid up the cost of deposits, costs of funds also increased. Customers and their communities suffered as well as taxpayers and the Federal government. America could only sustain an industry that promoted healthy competition. With a smaller number of profitable associations, the deregulation promulgated in the early 1980s would prosper. Excessive new rules and regulations would not be needed to supervise thrifts. These conditions would promote a healthy yet conservative savings system. There was no need to assume higher risk investments. Consolidation would precipitate the necessary staying power so that thrifts could withstand regional and national economic downturns.

Southwest Plan Mechanics

Southwest Plan transactions and FSLIC assistance packages completed through December 1988 included 217 thrifts with over $100 billion in assets. Each merger was different; however, a pattern emerged which embodied the following deal components:

> The failed savings and loan associations' negative net worth was covered by the FSLIC's issuance of ten year notes and the acquirer's cash investment.
>
> Purchasers were indemnified from unkown litigation and other liabilities.
>
> Yields and Real Estate Owned (REO) or foreclosed property were guaranteed by the FSLIC. For Texas thrifts, an investor's rate of return was determined by an already high Texas cost of funds.
>
> Net capital loss writedowns from asset sales were negotiated into profit sharing agreements with the FSLIC and the new ownership.
>
> Tax loss benefits were split at an agreed percentage between the FSLIC and the buyer.

After the first Southwest Plan transactions were announced, potential bidders for failed savings and loans were often questioned by their accountants about the collectibility of the FSLIC notes. Accounting industry experts argued that the FSLIC's practice of pledging notes to bolster insolvent thrifts was a course for disaster. With the first nine Southwest Plan deals through September 1988, over $5.1 billion of FSLIC promissory notes and $13.5 billion of additional FSLIC aid (capital loss and yield subsidiary coverage) were pledged by the FSLIC. As the pace of resolutions escalated in the fourth quarter of 1988, the General Accounting Office (GAO) and Congressional committees warned that the FHLBB should not be allowed to issue notes and sign assistance agreements independently. CEBA only provided for $10.8 billion over a three year period.

Lacking a specific Federal government guarantee for its notes, the FSLIC frequently paid a premium to provide assistance for Southwest thrift resolutions. Costs were decreased through note issuance because their tax exempt status attracted buyers willing to take smaller assistance amounts. Notes could also be transferred between institutions. Call provisions allowed the FSLIC to make payoffs when cash became available in the future.

Southwest Plan insolvent thrift case resolutions committed the FSLIC to compensate acquirers for future losses of failed institutions. Creative assistance arrangements were used as incentives. The FSLIC furnished coverage for capital losses resulting from problem asset sales or writedowns. It provided yield subsidies on nonperforming assets to guarantee a specific rate of return, indemnification against unknown litigation liabilities, and the purchase of certain impaired assets. These incentives were effected through the use of promissory notes, cash infusions, profit sharing agreements, capital loss coverages on selected assets, shared tax loss benefits, and the formation of collecting banks which are used as depositories for bad loans and real estate owned. The FSLIC almost always acquired equity interests, including stock or stock warrants or a specified share of the profits, in the buyers.

The problem with these creative financing techniques and guarantees was that future conditions could vary negatively from the time the resolution was consummated. Agreements with intricate accounting measures could increase FSLIC payouts to meet obligations under the settlements. The FSLIC has little control over the timing of cash outlays under guarantee provisions. Cost estimates were based upon the failed thrifts repaying their loans immediately, when in fact the repayments, spread over many years, would result in much higher costs on the guaranteed loans. Tax loss sharing arrangements also added to the total taxpayer cost. The Southwest Plan's demise was caused by the insufficient resources allocated to the FHLBB to eliminate the capital deficiency at Texas thrifts.

The Bush Administration Plan

In February 1989, President George Bush outlined a plan to rescue failed FSLIC-insured thrifts. The initial $90 billion plan called for (1) an immediate halt to all uncompleted Southwest Plan transactions, (2) higher thrift and bank deposit insurance premiums for a three year period, (3) tighter supervisory standards, (4) a 6 percent FDIC capital requirement by 1991, (5) replacement of the FHLBB by a single chairman, (6) Treasury Department control of thrift institution chartering and regulatory activity, and (7) the immediate use of FDIC personnel for FSLIC case resolutions.

Bond sales would raise $50 billion over a three year period for the to-be-created Resolution Funding Corporation (RFC). Another innovation, the Resolution Trust Corporation (RTC), would hold failed thrift assets. The Treasury Secretary, Federal Reserve Board Chairman, and the U.S. Comptroller General would comprise the three member RTC board. The board would operate for five years to liquidate thrift assets in a cost effective manner.

The $50 billion bond total would be retired by zero coupon bonds purchased with thrift and FHLB System funds. The liquidation of FSLIC receivership assets and taxpayer funds would cover interest charges. The RFC bonds would be issued in amounts of $10 billion in 1989, $25 billion in 1990, and $15 billion in 1991.

A critical part of the plan was the use of the FDIC to assume supervisory control of the FSLIC failure resolution function. The FSLIC immediately contracted the FDIC to act as conservator for insolvent thrifts. A conservatorship allows current thrift management to remain, although under strict controls. Unlike an FSLIC receivership, a conservatorship leaves the insolvent thrift, and not the FSLIC/FDIC, defendants to any litigation that might arise. Over three hundred insolvent savings and loans were expected to eventually become FDIC conservatorships. The FDIC involvement also signaled the end of FSLIC note usage for thrift merger acquisitions. Until new congressional funding was approved, no pending Southwest Plan deals would be completed.

The FDIC should play a major role in the thrift industry's bailout. President Bush's plan was simply a proposal. Congress must ultimately decide the final form of the solution. That compromise will include input from the FDIC, the FSLIC, the thrift and banking industries, the private sector, and Congress.

Chapter 3.

THE FEDERAL HOME LOAN BANK BOARD (FHLBB)

The Godfather of the Savings and Loan Industry

The Federal Home Loan Bank Board adopts the regulations that guide the Federal Home Loan Bank System. These policies promote efficiency in its operation and ensure the safety and soundness of the nation's thrift institutions. The Bank Board consists of two elements: a governing panel that makes policy and an independent federal agency that implements Bank Board policy by regulating, monitoring, and supervising the savings and loan industry.

The Bank Board panel is composed of three members appointed by the President and confirmed by the Senate to serve four year terms. The President designates one member of the panel as chairman. No more than two board members may belong to the same political party.

The agency is self-supporting and uses no tax revenues. Its operating costs are paid from a Treasury account funded by assessments on the 12 District Banks and the FSLIC. The District Banks, in turn, charge the individual thrift institutions fees for examination audits.

The Bank Board members meet in formal session as often as necessary, usually once a week. During these meetings, the Board

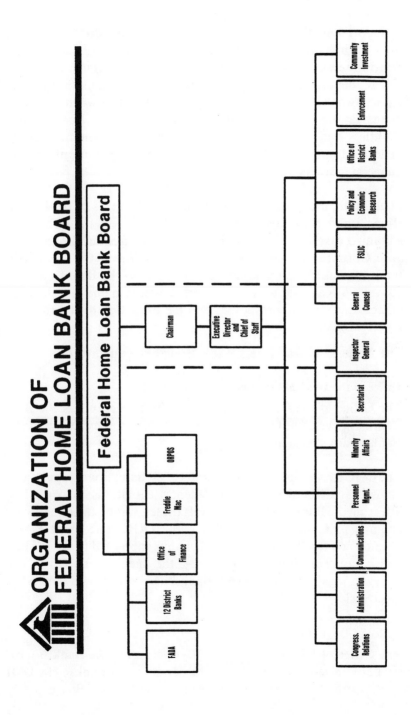

ORGANIZATION OF
FEDERAL HOME LOAN BANK BOARD

Federal Home Loan Bank Board

Chairman

Executive Director and Chief of Staff

FADA

12 District Banks

Office of Finance

Freddie Mac

ORPOS

Congress. Relations

Administration

Communications

Personnel Mgmt.

Minority Affairs

Secretariat

Inspector General

General Counsel

FSLIC

Policy and Economic Research

Office of District Banks

Enforcement

Community Investment

adopts or amends regulations affecting the entire thrift industry and rules on individual thrift matters. Bank Board decisions include creating new savings institutions with federal charters, granting new FSLIC deposit insurance, and advising associations on financial reporting and investments. The Bank Board decides when to close or merge failing institutions. In any single year, the Board makes countless decisions that affect the safety and soundness of the Federal Home Loan Bank System's member institutions and the financial markets in general.

In addition, the Bank Board members are directors of the Federal Home Loan Mortgage Corporation. They direct the policy and administrative decisions for the Federal Savings and Loan Insurance Corporation, and oversee the regulation of the 12 District Banks. Specific responsibility for carrying out the Board's numerous missions and supporting its needs is vested in one or more of its offices. Each office is responsible to the Bank Board Chairman.

The Federal Home Loan Bank Board Organization

Office of the General Counsel

The Office of the General Counsel (OGC) functions as the Bank Board's lawyer. The Office employs over 100 attorneys to handle the Bank Board's legal affairs.

The OGC staff prepare the final drafts of all Bank Board regulations, advise Bank Board members on agency regulations, interpret laws affecting the Bank System, and draft the legislation the Bank Board submits to Congress. In addition, the OGC staff prepare legal opinions on thrift institution applications submitted to the FHLBB and conduct all litigation involving the agency. The Office also provides legal services to other Bank Board offices and the FSLIC receiverships.

Office of District Banks

The Office of District Banks (ODB) operates as the Bank Board's primary liaison with the 12 Federal Home Loan Banks. The ODB works with the District Banks to implement Bank Board policy, reviews the District Banks' performance and operating procedures, and monitors the District Banks' processing of thrift institutions' applications.

One of the ODB's primary responsibilities is to oversee the District Banks' operations to ensure conformity with Bank Board regulations and policies. The ODB evaluates budget requests and monitors service charges to member institutions. The Office supervises the appointment of public interest directors and conducts the elections of other directors for Bank System member institutions.

The ODB's Application Analysis Division reviews and recommends final action on thrift institutions' applications. The Bank Board must approve applications for federal savings and loan associations or savings banks, branch offices, FSLIC insurance, and thrift institution mergers. The division further reviews applications that the District Banks have approved under FHLBB authority.

The Office of District Banks collects financial and operating data on the 12 District Banks. The information is incorporated into the Bank Board's comprehensive financial reports and the District Banks' combined financial statements.

Office of Policy and Economic Research
The Office of Policy and Economic Research (OPER) studies the financial marketplace to advise the Bank Board on regulatory policies. The OPER reviews the past by evaluating the results of previous policies under historical conditions. The future is simulated to determine what would happen if the Bank Board followed a given policy under various economic circumstances. Such information is vital to the Bank Board's understanding of how regulations have affected the District Banks and member thrift institutions in the past and how proposed regulations might affect them in the future.

The Office's staff members review, analyze, and aggregate monthly and quarterly reports filed by every FSLIC-insured savings institution. The resulting compilations, along with special surveys that the OPER conducts, give a comprehensive picture of the housing finance industry. To gauge future economic trends and provide tools for planning, the OPER uses a variety of econometric techniques and computerized models.

Office of Community Investment

The Office of Community Investment (OCI) seeks to stimulate thrift industry investment in older communities. Created in 1977, the OCI expanded programs begun in the 1960s by the Bank Board's former Office of Housing and Urban Affairs. One of the most important of OCI's programs has been the Community Investment Fund. In its five years of operation from 1978 to 1983, the Community Investment Fund helped underwrite the construction of 571,585 housing units in older urban and rural communities. In 1984, following the termination of the national program, the Bank Board gave each District Bank the option of initiating such a program on its own.

The Office of Community Investment supplies training materials and technical assistance to the District Banks to encourage the growth, safety, and soundness of minority-owned savings institutions. The OCI promotes industry compliance of civil rights and consumer legislation by guiding the District Banks' supervisory agent investigations of complaints against individual savings and loan associations.

The OCI coordinates the Bank Board's technical assistance to other nations. It administers a contract funded by the U.S. Agency for International Development to assist other countries in developing their own thrift and home financing systems. The OCI also makes arrangements for numerous foreign visitors to the Bank Board.

Office of Enforcement

Created in 1986, the Office of Enforcement (OE) ensures that FSLIC-insured member association managers, directors, and other personnel comply with FHLBB regulations for sound operating practices. The Office accomplishes its mission by issuing temporary or final cease and desist orders. OE removes negligent officers and directors after executing complex settlement agreements. In the most serious cases, the OE establishes conservatorships or receiverships.

When it cannot find a remedy on an informal or consent basis, the OE prosecutes such matters in administrative enforcement proceedings and U.S. District Courts. To determine if formal action is warranted, the OE investigates suspected violations of unsound practices by associations, thrift officials, or persons doing business with the institutions.

The OE serves as counsel to the supervisory agents at the District Banks and the Office of Regulatory Policy, Oversight, and Supervision. In addition, OE attorneys prepare detailed criminal referral letters to the U.S. Department of Justice when information developed during investigations reveals evidence that crimes have occurred.

Office of Congressional Relations

The Office of Congressional Relations (OCR) serves as the primary link between the Bank Board and Congress. The OCR works closely with the Senate Banking, Housing, and Urban Affairs Committee and the House Banking, Finance, and Urban Affairs Committee. These groups generally handle legislation affecting the Bank System.

Among its other duties, the OCR coordinates the submission of the agency's budget to Congress. Funds for the Bank Board's operating expenses come from the industry it regulates. Congress does not appropriate any funds from the U.S. Treasury for Bank Board use. However, the House and Senate Appropriations Subcommittees on HUD-Independent Agencies review the Bank Board's annual budget. Congress approves an authorization bill containing limits on the total funds the Bank Board may spend.

Communications Office

The Communications Office informs the news media and the public about Bank Board policies, programs, and decisions. It circulates information through press releases, press conferences, and Bank Board staff interviews. The Office distributes texts of all Bank Board regulations and public FHLBB member testimony. The Communications Office handles countless telephone and letter inquires from the news media and general public. The Office also provides graphic, photographic, audiovisual, and video services to the Bank Board.

Office of the Secretariat, Planning, and Management Coordination

The Office of the Secretariat, Planning, and Management Coordination maintains the official records of the Bank Board, the former Home Owners' Loan Corporation, and the Federal Home Loan Bank Administration. The Office organizes Bank Board meeting agendas and coordinates transmission of staff papers. The Office prepares minutes and records decisions by transmitting new regulations to the Office of the Federal Register for official publication. The Office staff briefs new Bank Board members, advises the Bank Board on Sunshine Act compliance, and releases information under the Freedom of Information and Privacy Acts. It maintains a research facility that the public uses to inspect records and documents. The Office coordinates Bank Board planning meetings and provides interoffice coordination of issues being developed for Bank Board consideration. It prepares and records federal thrift charters, FSLIC insurance certificates, and installations of the Federal Home Loan Bank directors.

Office of Inspector General

The Office of Inspector General (OIG) functions as the Bank System's internal watchdog. At the Bank Board's direction, the OIG conducts audits and investigations within the Bank Board, the FSLIC, the District Banks, the Office of Finance, and the Neighborhood Reinvestment Corporation. The OIG promotes efficiency and economy while auditing to uncover fraud or abuse. The OIG administers contracts with the District Banks' outside auditors and serves as liaison between the Bank Board and the U.S. General Accounting Office.

Personnel Management Office

The Personnel Management Office (PMO) advises Bank Board members and staff regarding personnel management practices. The PMO develops programs for recruitment while conforming to the regulations of the Bank Board and the U.S. Office of Personnel Management. The PMO also coordinates staff training programs and other developmental activities.

Office of Minority Affairs

The Office of Minority Affairs works closely with the Personnel Management Office, Bank Board members, and other Bank Board offices to develop and implement the FHLBB's equal employment opportunity (EEO) policies.

Administration Office

The Administration Office helps develop and deliver many services needed by the FHLBB and the FSLIC. These services include accounting, budget preparation, data processing, and facilities management.

The Administration Office's Information Systems Division designs and operates the FHLBB computer systems. The Bank Board, the FSLIC, and the District Banks process and store vast amounts of financial data generated by the FHLBB System. The Administration Office's Budget Division plans, develops, and controls the Bank Board's budget. The Office helps implement programs mandated by the federal Office of Management and Budget (OMB). The Controller's Division prepares bills for the agency's services, receives and disburses agency funds, and safeguards securities and other valuable documents. The Controller's Division also makes arrangements for personnel traveling on agency business.

The Federal Savings and Loan Advisory Council

Congress established the Federal Savings and Loan Advisory Council in 1935. Although it is not part of the Bank Board, the Council brings the concerns of the thrift industry to the Board's attention, providing a bridge between the regulated and the regulator.

The Council's 24 voting members represent a broad cross section of the thrift and housing industries and the public. The Council includes one member from each of the 12 District Banks, elected annually by each District Bank's board of directors. The Bank

Board annually appoints the other 12 members to represent the public interest. The Council meets at least twice a year to consider major issues facing the savings and loan industry and to make recommendations to the Bank Board.

Chapter 4.

THE DISTRICT BANKS

District Banks' Purpose

The District Banks are the thrift industry's bankers. Whereas most commercial banks rely on one of the 12 Federal Reserve Banks for bank-like services, the majority of savings and loan associations and savings banks turn to one of the 12 Federal Home Loan Banks for financial and technical assistance. The District Banks link the Bank System's other two key elements: the Bank Board in Washington, and the more than 3,000 federally chartered and state-chartered savings and loan associations and savings banks throughout the United States.

The District Banks opened for business in October 1932, at the lowest point of the Great Depression under the Federal Home Loan Bank Act. The Bank Board created 12 District Banks, now located in Boston, New York, Pittsburgh, Atlanta, Cincinnati, Indianapolis, Chicago, Des Moines, Dallas, Topeka, San Francisco, and Seattle.

The District Banks' primary mission is to channel money into the housing finance industry by making loans to individual thrift institutions. Thrifts use the funds to make loans to home buyers or to meet demands for deposit withdrawals. The District Banks work to balance funds according to local needs, transferring money from areas with surplus deposits to areas with insufficient savings to meet

FEDERAL HOME LOAN BANK SYSTEM

mortgage demands. The 12 Bank network is thus responsive to economic variations in different regions of the United States.

The District Banks normally make advances available at interest rates that are lower than those of the commercial market, particularly on longer-term funds. This practice helps member savings institutions manage interest rate gaps (the differences between the rates institutions pay on borrowed funds and rates earned on funds invested). District Banks provide thrifts with check clearing, safekeeping of securities, demand and time deposit accounts, technical assistance, economic analysis, and access to the federal funds markets. By design, the District Banks are profit-making intermediaries which provide earnings that can return dividends to the Banks' stockholders. By examining and supervising member institutions, they ensure that thrifts comply with federal law and Bank Board regulations.

Structure of the District Banks

The District Banks are hybrid organizations, wholly owned by their members: savings and loan associations, savings banks, and insurance companies. However, they are ultimately controlled by the Federal government. Every federally chartered thrift institution must become a member of a District Bank. Membership is optional for state-chartered institutions, but nearly all of them become members because the FSLIC will not insure any nonmember institution. A thrift joins the District Bank that serves the state in which the thrift's home office or principal place of business is located.

A thrift institution becomes a member of a District Bank, and hence the Bank System, by purchasing the District Bank's stock. Unlike most common stock, District Bank stock is not traded on any exchange. The Banks sell stock only to their member institutions. A member institution of one District Bank cannot buy stock in another District Bank, nor can the District Banks buy each other's stock. Moreover, a member that finds it holds more than the required amount of District Bank stock may sell the excess back only to that District Bank. (On rare occasions, some District Banks have permitted their stock to be exchanged directly between member institutions within the same district.) Each share of stock entitles its owner to one vote in the District Bank Corporation. To prevent the largest institutions from dominating the District Banks, no one institution is permitted more votes than the average number of shares held by all members in that institution's home state.

Each District Bank is governed by a board of at least fourteen directors: two directors are designated by the Bank Board each year to serve as the District Bank's chairman and vice-chairman. The District Bank's member institutions elect eight of the directors and the FHLBB in Washington appoints six. In districts that include more than five states, the Bank Board may increase the number of District Bank Board directors as long as there are no more than thirteen elected members. The elected members should outnumber the appointed members by a ratio of four to three. Although each District Bank has more locally elected directors than federally appointed directors, the appointed directors serve four year terms, compared with two years for the elected directors.

The elected directors are chosen by state. Member institutions in each state are entitled to at least one director, but not more than six directors. The number of elected directors is proportionate to the percentage of the District Bank's stock held by member thrift institutions in the state. The Bank Board chooses the directors it appoints, called public interest directors, to represent various community groups, including business, law, academia, and religion. The directors must reside in the district they serve.

The FHLBB has final authority over the actions of each District Bank's board of directors, such as adopting the District Bank's annual budget. The Bank Board has empowered the District Banks with authority to set capital stock dividend rates and to appoint District Bank officers. In theory, nearly every District Bank action technically comes under Bank Board review. In practice, the FHLBB delegates substantial operating authority to the Banks.

The most important delegated functions involve supervisory responsibilities. The Bank Board designates District Bank employees as supervisory agents. They are responsible for instituting corrective measures at thrift institutions and for providing day-to-day supervisory oversight. The District Bank's President usually serves as the Bank Board's principal supervisory agent (PSA). He holds district level authority to approve certain member institution applications and enforce federal regulations. Because of this position's importance, the District Bank President, although appointed by the District Bank's board of directors, must be approved by the Bank Board.

The Bank Board gives District Banks broad authority for providing member thrift services. While functioning within FHLBB guidelines, the District Banks develop services to satisfy local thrift industry needs. As long as the Banks meet the Bank Board's basic requirements, District Bank boards of directors can determine additional member services and associated charges.

Bank System Offices

The following four offices are funded by the District Banks to serve specific Bank System needs.

Office of Finance

The Office of Finance (OF) issues consolidated debt, manages investments, clears securities, conducts financial planning and research, and provides support services to aid District Bank financial management. The Office's director is responsible to the Bank Board and the 12 District Bank Presidents. The OF acts as liaison between the District Banks, the FSLIC, and the Bank Board.

As fiscal agent for the District Banks, the OF sells consolidated bonds and notes. The bonds have terms from one year to ten years and the discount notes have terms from one month to one year. The OF investigates alternative debt sources to meet District Bank needs. For instance, during the period from 1984 to 1986, the OF several times reopened previously issued bonds for sale as a means of satisfying the District Banks' demand for additional maturities. The OF placed issues in the Eurodollar market and issued bonds denominated in yen and European Currency Units.

The OF's research and product development goes beyond the search for alternative debt instruments. The OF implements District Bank policies, programs, and reporting systems. These include futures options and cash hedging, interest rate swaps, and asset-liability management. The OF also undertakes financial research projects at the request of the Bank Board, the District Banks, and the FSLIC.

Office of Regulatory Policy, Oversight, and Supervision

The Office of Regulatory Policy, Oversight, and Supervision (ORPOS), located in Washington, D.C., was established by the Bank Board on October 1, 1986. It assumed the functions and personnel of the former Office of Examinations and Supervision (OES), which was then abolished. Like the other Bank System offices, the ORPOS is not an office of the Federal government. The transformation ended civil service constraints on staffing, salaries, and personnel practices. One year after the privatization of the OES, federal OES thrift examiners transferred from the employ of the Federal government to the District Bank jurisdiction.

The ORPOS monitors the activities of Bank System examiners, who ensure that individual thrift institutions follow federal law and Bank Board regulations. Bank System examiners monitor the books and operations of all FSLIC-insured savings institutions. Each institution must pay a fee for its examination.

Bank System examiners bear sole responsibility for auditing federally chartered institutions. Federal and state examiners work side-by-side to examine state-chartered thrifts in more than half the states, undertaking joint examinations and issuing joint reports. In a few states, federal and state examiners concurrently audit institutions, sharing the workload but issuing separate reports. In other states, federal and state examiners take turns conducting examinations and share the results.

If an examination uncovers a discrepancy, a supervisory agent from the District Bank works with the institution to solve the problem. This is usually handled in informal meetings between supervisory officials and the association's management. If necessary, the Bank Board may issue a cease-and-desist order, which the institution must obey. The ORPOS may recommend other corrective action, including removing a thrift institution's officers or directors. The ORPOS also helps arrange the merger of a troubled thrift with a healthy financial institution. By taking such action early, the ORPOS can sometimes prevent the need to involve the FSLIC.

The ORPOS also instructs Bank System staff regarding thrift institution compliance with Bank Board regulations and draft examination and supervision procedures. The ORPOS helps formulate proposed regulations dealing with the examination and supervisory process, thrift industry operation, and accounting standard determinations.

FHLB System Publication Corporation

The FHLB System Publication Corporation, established in August 1984 and operated by the District Banks, publishes the Bank System's bimonthly magazine, *Outlook of the Federal Home Loan Bank System*. The corporation's headquarters are located in Washington, D.C.

FHLB System Office of Education

The Office of Education provides comprehensive specialized training to Bank Board and District Bank employees. Programs help managerial staff learn new policies and procedures to become more effective. Established in June 1984, the Office of Education maintains its headquarters near Dallas, Texas. In 1985 the Office began training examiners, who were transferred that year from the federal civil service system to the District Bank staffs.

Chapter 5.

THE FEDERAL SAVINGS AND LOAN INSURANCE CORPORATION (FSLIC)

A Brief History

"Your Savings are Insured to $100,000." More than 100 million American savers trust these words and the guarantee they represent. The gold and black emblem indicating a thrift institution's membership in the FSLIC has symbolized safety since the insurance corporation's creation in 1934.

To the general public, the FSLIC is by far the most visible federal presence in the thrift institutions system. The FSLIC's primary mission is to ensure consumer confidence in savings and loans by guaranteeing that insured savings will be available to depositors even if savings institutions become insolvent. The FSLIC has succeeded: despite periodic failures of savings institutions, no saver has ever lost a penny of FSLIC-insured deposits.

Congress created the FSLIC to restore the public confidence lost in the chaos and panic of the Great Depression, when many thrifts failed. The National Housing Act of 1934 established the FSLIC as a permanent government instrumentality and placed it under the supervision and authority of the Federal Home Loan Bank Board. President Roosevelt signed the legislation into law on June 27, 1934,

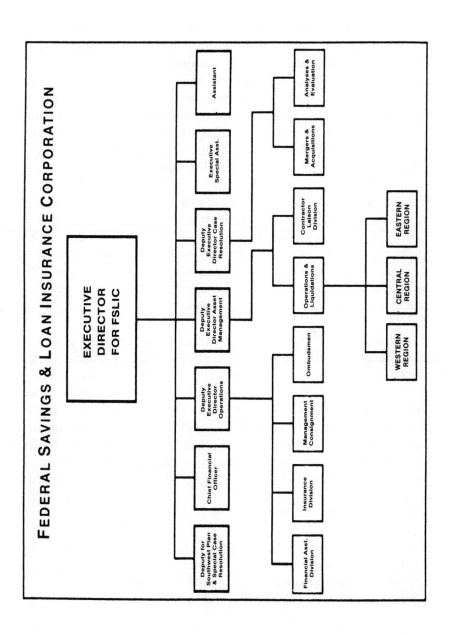

FEDERAL SAVINGS & LOAN INSURANCE CORPORATION

EXECUTIVE DIRECTOR FOR FSLIC

- Deputy for Southwest Plan & Special Case Resolution
- Chief Financial Officer
- Deputy Executive Director Operations
- Deputy Executive Director Asset Management
- Deputy Executive Director Case Resolution
- Executive Special Asst.
- Assistant

Chief Financial Officer:
- Financial Asst. Division
- Insurance Division
- Management Consignment
- Ombudsmen

Deputy Executive Director Asset Management / Case Resolution:
- Operations & Liquidations
- Contractor Liaison Division
- Mergers & Acquisitions
- Analyses & Evaluation

Operations & Liquidations:
- WESTERN REGION
- CENTRAL REGION
- EASTERN REGION

and on September 29, 1934, the Bank Board approved insurance for the first ten savings associations to be covered.

The savings institutions industry resisted the new insurance. All federally chartered associations by law had to carry it. However, it was optional for state-chartered institutions. Many savings and loans initially refused to register for the insurance because of the associated federal regulation. By mid-1936, only 237 state-chartered associations along with 1,099 federally chartered associations held FSLIC coverage. It was not until 1940 that half of all savings associations held FSLIC insurance, and not until 1951 that FSLIC-insured thrifts outnumbered non-FSLIC-insured thrifts.

The FSLIC began operations in 1934 with $100 million in capital which the FSLIC raised by selling its stock to the Home Owners' Loan Corporation (HOLC). When the HOLC was phased out in 1948, the FSLIC stock was transferred to the Secretary of the Treasury. In 1950 the FSLIC began to buy back the stock, using 50 percent of its income each year for that purpose. By 1958 the FSLIC had repurchased all of the outstanding stock.

Today, although it receives some income from the earnings on its investment portfolio, the FSLIC receives funding primarily from the insurance premiums levied on insured institutions. In 1934 the initial premium rate was 0.25 percent of an institution's total deposits. The next year the premium was reduced to 0.125 percent. Since 1950 each insured thrift has paid a regular premium of approximately 0.083 percent of total deposits. In 1985 the Bank Board exercised its authority to make special premium assessments totaling as much as 0.125 percent of deposits per year. It imposed quarterly assessments of approximately 0.031 percent of insured deposits in addition to the normal premium.

The amount of insurance coverage has gradually been increased. In 1934 the insurance limit per individual account was established at $5,000. The limit was increased to $10,000 in 1950, $15,000 in 1966, $20,000 in 1969, $40,000 in 1974, and $100,000 in 1980.

Adjusting to Thrift Industry Demands

While the savings and loan industry's needs have changed over the years, so did the activities of the FSLIC to meet those requirements. During the FSLIC's early years, the primary focus was to promote deposit insurance. To accomplish this task, field offices were set up around the country. Due to the unstable economic conditions of the 1930s, a division was established to manage liquidating institutions.

By 1947, market conditions had changed. With the number of insured institutions steadily increasing, the FSLIC organizationally adjusted to prepare for the future demands. The FSLIC had evolved into the following divisions:

- Claims and Adjustment,
- Liquidation and Recoveries,
- Underwriting and Rehabilitation,
- Comptroller, and
- Operating Analysis.

By establishing this structure, the FSLIC separated its major responsibilities into three functional areas: default prevention, liquidation management, and account insurance education. Field personnel supported the Washington Office in these activities as well as marketing insurance protection.

During 1965 the activities of the FSLIC were realigned once again into three separate divisions, each reporting to the FSLIC Director:

1. The Insurance Settlement Division was responsible for insurance payments and educational programs about account insurance.

2. The Problem and Rehabilitation Division was accountable for close liaison with the FHLBB Office of Examinations and Supervision. It developed and implemented default prevention methods in specific cases.

3. The Liquidation Division, both directly and through a field staff, was responsible for the management and liquidation of assets acquired from failed institutions.

The FSLIC Organizational Structure Today

The organizational structure of the FSLIC remained relatively constant until the early 1980s. Since that time, the FSLIC has evolved into an organization with five major divisions: the Operations and Liquidations Division (OLD), the Insurance Division (INS), the Analysis and Evaluation Division (AED), the Financial Assistance Division (FAD), and the Mergers and Acquisitions Division (MAD).

Mergers and Acquisitions Division (MAD)

When a supervisory case is forwarded to the FSLIC from a District Bank, the Mergers and Acquisitions Division attempts to find potential acquirers for insolvent thrifts primarily by arranging bidders' conferences. In recent years, as the caseload mounted and resources became scarce, the MAD redoubled its efforts to find assisted solutions to these cases. A marketing unit was formed with a number of professionals that aggressively canvass nationwide for potential merger partners for insolvent institutions. Besides thrift candidates, non-thrift institutions like bank holding companies, insurance companies, mortgage companies, and industrial corporations as well as private investors, are approached to effect case resolution. The campaign to solve cases intensified since the first FSLIC CEBA recapitalization plan became effective in 1987.

Analysis and Evaluation Division (AED)

The second key link in the case resolution process is the Analysis and Evaluation Division. This Division provides quantitative analysis support to other operating divisions to find only the most cost effective solutions. The AED estimates costs of liquidations versus assisted mergers. Sophisticated computer models analyze various interest rate scenarios with other pertinent data to determine the lowest resolution cost. In effect, the AED acts as an investment advisor for the FSLIC.

The AED has an ambitious schedule to cope with the anticipated heavy case flows. The Division constructed and implemented a data base and case tracking system, developed innovative structures for case resolutions, and expanded the scope and sophistication of financial and interest rate forecasting models. These changes have made the Division more effective in achieving mission goals.

Financial Assistance Division (FAD)

The Financial Assistance Division has the responsibility for administering all assistance agreements and related contracts arising from assistance plans approved by the Bank Board. The Division enforces compliance with standards, monitors agreements, makes payments through the controller as required, and contracts for mandated internal audits. The FAD operates through two branches: Contract Management and Treasury Compliance.

The FAD has joint responsibility for oversight, control, and monitoring of the Management Consignment Program and the Southwest Plan, which includes both conservatorships and pass-through receiverships. Primary accountability of these functions was consolidated into an MCP Division. This unit functions as an intermediary between Bank Board personnel and District Bank staff, who have delegated authority over the daily operations of the MCP thrifts. The unit serves as an early warning beacon for troublesome issues, assists in establishing policy guidelines, and handles all other incidental activities relating to MCPs at the Washington level.

Insurance Division (INS)

The Insurance Division plays an important FSLIC role by managing account insurance programs, including fee structure, risk analysis, preparation of payment procedures, conduct of payouts, and claims handling during and after a payout. During the 1980-1987 period, the Division's resources were severely taxed through the liquidation of more than 50 institutions. The liquidation schedule for 1988 and beyond anticipated closing or merging hundreds of insolvent institutions. This ambitious program depends upon the passage of further recapitalization legislation. One of the most critical obstacles to an even heavier liquidation schedule is the labor intensive nature of the function. This constraint is being addressed by adding FSLIC and FDIC personnel, which will increase capacity to meet heavy caseload demands over the next few years.

Operations and Liquidations Division (OLD)

The Operations and Liquidations Division provides liaison between divisions of the FHLBB System to ensure coordination of the various FSLIC takeover functions upon a thrift institution failure. The OLD plans and arranges takeover logistic teams and conducts all pass-through and liquidating receivership takeover transactions. It maintains adequate control of the defaulted institution while minimizing disruption and inconvenience to the depositors and the general public.

The OLD assures that each receivership is operated as a business, and that fiduciary responsibilities of the FSLIC as Receiver are prudently upheld. To ensure nationwide consistency and control, the OLD develops the policies and procedures necessary to standardize receivership operations. Each receivership's management is monitored to provide an efficient yet effective liquidation process. Cost conscious operations are emphasized to comply with established policy and federal regulatory requirements. Training programs for receivership staff ensure effective implementation of liquidation procedures.

The OLD monitors the administrative claims process and the adjudication of creditor claims to ensure consistent nationwide claims treatment for all uninsured depositors of failed thrift institutions.

When Savings Institutions Have Failed in the Past

To minimize losses to the insurance fund, the Federal Home Loan Bank Board; the Bank System's Office of Regulatory Policy, Oversight, and Supervision; and the regulatory staffs of the Federal Home Loan Banks carefully monitor trends within the thrift industry. They ensure that all thrifts operate in a safe and sound manner. Even with careful monitoring and regulation, some savings institutions cannot meet their obligations. When this happens, the Federal Home Loan Bank Board declares the institution insolvent. Utilizing FSLIC receivership status, the Bank Board transfers the responsibility for managing and liquidating the thrift to the FSLIC.

Section 406(f) of the National Housing Act of 1934 empowers the FSLIC to use the least expensive way of carrying out its primary obligation of guaranteeing that depositors do not lose insured savings. The FSLIC is authorized to provide loans or contributions to troubled institutions and acquire assets or liabilities, as long as the estimated costs of doing so are lower than the costs of liquidating the institutions. The FSLIC can financially assist the merger, acquisition, or consolidation of failed thrifts into other institutions.

As an alternative to arranging a merger or acquisition, the FSLIC can give direct financial assistance to the troubled institution. The sharp increase in problem cases that resulted from the abnormally high interest rates of the early 1980s led the FSLIC to develop the income capital certificate (ICC) program in 1981. Under this program, a problem thrift sells ICCs to the FSLIC, with an agreement that the institution eventually will repurchase the ICCs. Although the FSLIC can pay cash for the ICCs, it is more likely to give the thrift a promissory note. The FSLIC promises to pay a fixed amount of money at a specified future date, usually five years. In buying ICCs, the FSLIC acquires an equity interest in the institution. The institution can list outstanding ICCs as part of its regulatory capital. At maturity, the FSLIC is obligated to pay the face amount of the promissory note or negotiate another note. The institution does not have to begin repaying the ICCs until an operating profit is realized.

The Garn-St Germain Depository Institutions Act of 1982 authorized distressed thrifts to issue net worth certificates (NWCs) to the FSLIC in exchange for the FSLIC's promissory notes. A thrift may use a promissory note in computing net worth, thus raising the thrift's capital level and buying time to strengthen the thrift's financial base. The FSLIC is also empowered to convert troubled institutions from mutual to stock ownership as a means of infusing new capital.

When a troubled FSLIC-insured thrift institution encounters the imminent danger of default and requires FSLIC financial assistance as part of a supervisory-arranged solution, the Office of Regulatory Policy, Oversight, and Supervision contacts the FSLIC's Mergers and Acquisitions Division to devise a way of dealing with the problem thrift that minimizes insurance fund costs. The MAD strives to make each solution fit the particular circumstances. Sometimes, the MAD arranges for the FSLIC to pay a healthy institution to take over the failed institution and all its related problems. Frequently, the Division recommends that the FSLIC take over the failed institution's worst assets or guarantee the acquiring institution a certain spread or return, on those assets. At other times, the MAD prefers that the FSLIC indemnify the acquiring association against any losses that might arise out of lawsuits stemming from the merger or acquisition. The FSLIC can also reimburse the surviving institution for losses that might be uncovered as the failed institution's books are analyzed.

If a merger is the answer, the Division tries to find a merger partner in the same state that is a like-kind of financial intermediary (i.e., savings and loan association or savings bank) as the failed institution. There have been times when this has not been possible. In May 1981 the Bank Board began allowing mergers and acquisitions by out-of-state institutions when no in-state partner could be found. In 1982 the Bank Board allowed the first FSLIC-assisted acquisition by a company outside the thrift industry.

The first question to be answered when a thrift fails is whether the Mergers and Acquisitions Division can find an alternative to liquidation. If it can, and the Bank Board approves, the case moves to the FSLIC's Financial Assistance Division, which oversees the implementation of the solution. If the Mergers and Acquisitions Division recommends liquidation, the case moves to the FSLIC's Insurance Division for payment of insured savings to depositors. When the FSLIC has no other choice but to liquidate a failed savings and loan association or savings bank, the Insurance and the Operations and Liquidations divisions seize the institution and pay the depositors.

Seizure of a failed savings institution is a complex operation, which the Bank Board must carry out precisely and secretly. Secrecy is important to avoid saver panic, last minute maneuvers by the thrift's managers to better their own financial positions, and the destruction of records. Takeover usually occurs just before closing time. FSLIC team members enter the insolvent institution's home office and all branch offices and present the institution's senior manager on the premises with the Bank Board's written order of seizure. The written order may appoint the FSLIC as Receiver to dispose of the institution, or it may appoint a conservator to conserve the institution's remaining assets until a permanent solution can be found. Normally, the Bank Board relieves the failed association's senior managers of their duties immediately. The seizure team seals the doors and federal officials explain what has occurred to the association's staff.

The managers of any institution that the FSLIC seizes are generally well aware of the institution's financial problems. Bank Board officials typically have spent months or even years working with the thrift's managers in an effort to resolve the insolvency. Nonetheless, the moment of actual takeover almost always comes as a shock to the institution and the community it serves. If an association is seized on a Friday afternoon, its insured savings, including interest which stops being paid on the day of seizure, will probably be available to depositors the next Monday morning.

Once the payout orders are drawn, the Insurance Division returns funds to depositors. The FSLIC issues checks directly, drawing on an account established at a Federal Home Loan Bank, or indirectly, by providing funds through a third party in a technique called transfer of accounts. Under the indirect method, the Insurance Division transfers the failed thrift's savings accounts to another insured savings institution (selected at a bidders' conference held just before or after the failed thrift is seized). The Insurance Division pays the acquiring institution the dollar value of the insured funds, less a premium of a few percentage points that the acquiring institution contributes. The transfer of accounts procedure offers a number of advantages to all parties. The acquiring institution may gain the savers from the failed institution as new customers; with them, it gains a new marketing area. The FSLIC saves the premium paid by the acquiring institution, and thus reduces the cost to the insurance fund. The savers receive immediate access to their accounts, up to the insurance limit. Depositors can either keep their accounts open with the acquiring institution or withdraw their money. If the savers keep their accounts in place, the accounts retain original interest rates and other terms. In many cases, the acquiring institution keeps the failed institution's office open, maintaining an important sense of continuity for the community.

In addition to the above methods of liquidation, the FSLIC has adopted another technique: the asset-backed transfer. An asset-backed transfer is a variation of the transfer-of-accounts method, whereby the FSLIC transfers the insured accounts to a newly created mutual thrift institution. To offset this liability on the new institution's balance sheet, the FSLIC purchases, at fair market value, the good assets from the closed institution and places them on the books of the new mutual association. The FSLIC may also purchase and transfer other good assets from any other receivership portfolio. This infusion of good assets typically makes the new thrift more attractive to potential acquirers in the future. When appropriate real estate assets cannot be found in other receiverships, the FSLIC places cash or notes into the new mutual association. Nonperforming assets remain with the receivership for disposition.

What Accounts Are Covered under FSLIC Deposit Insurance?

When an institution must be closed, the FSLIC follows its congressional mandate to pay insurance promptly. Most depositors have full access to their funds within one to two weeks. The FSLIC settles insurance most often by providing depositors with new accounts in amounts equal to their insured balances at the failed institution. With this method, another FSLIC-insured institution agrees to service the account and pay interest. When this settlement method is not practical, the account holder is provided with a check for the amount of the insured account balance. With either method, payment includes principal and all interest accrued through the date of closing up to the insurance limit.

The FSLIC promptly notifies each account holder by mail of the closing and method of insurance payment. General information is available immediately through television, newspapers, and radio. When a new account is provided as the method of settlement, most depositors have access to their funds on the next business day. When payment is made by check, most depositors receive insured funds within the first week after the closing.

If a depositor's funds exceed the insurance limit, the excess funds are uninsured. The depositor receives the insured funds upon completion of an insurance determination. For the uninsured portion, the depositor is entitled to a share of any proceeds from the liquidation of the failed institution's assets.

When one insured institution is merged into another insured institution, each account, including principal and interest, is assumed by the surviving institution. If a depositor has accounts in both institutions, assumed balances will be separately insured for six months or, in the case of certificate accounts, until the earliest maturity date.

The statutory insurance limit is $100,000. Federal deposit insurance is not determined on a per account basis, but instead by ownership category. A depositor can have more than $100,000 insurance coverage in a single institution as long as the funds qualify for additional coverage under separate ownership categories.

There are four categories of accounts used by individuals that are separately insured by the FSLIC. Depositors may have insured funds in each of the four categories in the same savings institution. For each category, the insurance limit is applied to the aggregate amount the owner(s) holds in savings accounts at the institution, regardless of the number of accounts or type of savings instrument (e.g., NOW, Money Market, or certificate of deposit). In the event of default, settlement of insurance is usually completed within ten days and includes both principal and interest accrued to the date of default up to the insurance maximum.

Individual Accounts

Individual (single ownership) accounts are insured up to $100,000 in the aggregate. For example, if a depositor has both a NOW account and a certificate of deposit in one name alone, the funds in these accounts would be added together and insured for a total of

$100,000. This category includes funds placed by agents or nominees, guardians or custodians (e.g., Uniform Gifts to Minors), sole proprietorships, and funds from accounts that fail to meet the qualifying requirements for separate coverage in other categories.

Joint Accounts
To qualify for separate insurance in the joint account category, all co-owners must possess equal withdrawal rights and must personally sign the signature card. Insurance is then determined by applying these two steps:

1. First, all joint accounts that are owned by the same combination of individuals are added together, and the combined total is insured to $100,000.

2. After step one has been completed, joint accounts involving different combinations of individuals are reviewed to determine the amount of each person's ownership interest in all joint accounts. Each owner's attributable interest in all joint accounts is calculated and the total is insured up to $100,000.

Both steps one and two are always applied so that no joint account (or multiple joint accounts with identical ownership) can be insured for over $100,000. No individual can be insured for over $100,000 in the joint account category. Insurance coverage is determined by actual ownership within account categories. Additionally, insurance coverage is not increased by rearranging the names of the owners or by changing the style of the names. The use of "or" versus "and" to join owners' names in a joint account title does not affect insurance coverage. If an account fails to qualify for separate coverage in the joint account category, the funds in the account will be treated as the individual funds of the co-owners. As such, each owner's attributable interest is added together with any other individually owned funds and the total is insured to $100,000.

Testamentary/Revocable Trust Accounts
Testamentary/revocable trust funds are insured for each owner to $100,000 per beneficiary only if the beneficiary is the owner's spouse, child, or grandchild. The signature card or other revocable trust documentation must evidence the owner's intention that upon his

death the funds belong to the beneficiary. (If these qualifying conditions are not met, the funds in the account(s) are considered to belong to the owner individually and are added to any other individual funds of the owner and are insured up to $100,000 in the aggregate. For example, a son could not designate his parent as the beneficiary of a testamentary/revocable trust account if he wanted to have separate insurance coverage in this category.) Testamentary/ revocable trust funds owned by a husband and wife, naming their two children as beneficiaries, can be insured up to $400,000. These funds could be in one account or in several accounts.

If a beneficiary of a testamentary/revocable trust is not the spouse, child, or grandchild of the owner, the funds attributable to the beneficiary are insured as the owner's individual funds. For example, if a man held recoverable trust funds for his mother and his daughter, the portion of the funds for his daughter would be insured separately in the testamentary/revocable trust account category. However, the funds held in trust for his mother (a nonqualifying beneficiary) would be aggregated with any other individual funds of the man and insured up to the $100,000 limit of the individual category.

Note that step-children, step-grandchildren, and adopted children and grandchildren are considered qualified beneficiaries.

In evaluating insurance coverage of a "living" trust account, it is necessary to identify whether a beneficiary will have immediate and complete control over the funds upon the owner's death. If the conditions of the trust fulfill the requirements for coverage as a testamentary/revocable trust account, the insurance limits are described above. Otherwise, the trust funds may be insured as the individual funds of the owner (grantor). As such, they are added to any individual funds of the owner and insured to a total of $100,000 in the individual category. An attorney should review trust documents to determine whether regulatory requirements are met.

Irrevocable Trusts

Irrevocable trusts are established by written instruments whereby the grantor contributes funds (or property) without retaining the power to revoke the trust. Common types of irrevocable trusts include those created by wills and many employee benefit plans (such as pension and profit sharing trusts). Also in this category are IRA and Keogh plans.

The ownership interest of each beneficiary in an irrevocable trust account is insured to $100,000 separately from other accounts held by the trustee, grantor, or beneficiary. However, to obtain coverage in this category, the value of the beneficiary's ownership interest must be ascertainable from the records of the institution or those of the trustee. The trust agreement must be valid under state law.

In cases where the beneficiary has an ownership interest in more than one trust agreement created by the same grantor, the ownership interests of the beneficiary in all accounts established under those trusts are added together and insured to a total of $100,000. With the exception of IRA and Keogh accounts, separate coverage cannot be obtained within this category when the same person is both grantor and beneficiary.

The existence of the trust relationship must be disclosed in the thrift institution's records. This is accomplished by disclosing in the account title that a trust relationship exists and by completion of an appropriate trust signature card. IRAs and Keoghs are insured separately from each other and any other individual or trust accounts of the beneficiaries. The combination of all IRA accounts owned by an individual in one institution is insured up to $100,000. Similarly, an individual's Keogh accounts are added together and insured up to $100,000.

Each beneficiary's ascertainable interest in a valid employee benefit trust account is insured up to $100,000. If a company establishes accounts for more than one plan (for example, a pension plan and a profit sharing plan) at the same institution for the same employees, the ownership interests of a participant in each plan are added together and insured to the $100,000 limit. As for all irrevocable trust accounts, documentation requirements must be met.

When the identity or quantifiable ownership interests of the beneficiaries cannot be determined, insurance coverage for the trust fund account(s) is limited to a total of $100,000. Common examples of this type of trust situation include health and welfare plans or scholarship funds where the exact beneficiaries and their ownership interests are not pre-determined.

Other Types of Accounts

Funds in accounts placed by guardians, conservators, or custodians (whether court-appointed or not) are insured to the actual owner and are added to any other individual accounts that owner may have at the institution. The fiduciary relationship must be disclosed in the records of the institution. Funds owned by an individual or entity and invested by an agent or nominee are added to any individual accounts of the principal (actual owner) and insured to $100,000 in the aggregate. Provided that the principal does not have any other individual accounts at the same institution, the funds of the principal are fully insured up to $100,000.

The insurance regulations allow an agent to place the funds of several principals into one account. Provided that proper disclosure has been made, the funds of each principal are separately insured. The agent's fiduciary capacity must be disclosed in the records of the institution. Although it is not required for the agent to identify the name and ownership interest of each principal in the institution records, these details must be ascertainable from records maintained in good faith and the ordinary course of business.

The accounts of a corporation, partnership, or unincorporated association are insured up to $100,000. To qualify for this coverage, the entity must be engaged in an independent activity, which is defined as "any activity other than one directed solely at increasing insurance coverage." Note that accounts owned by the same entity but earmarked for different purposes are not separately insured but, rather, are added together and insured up to $100,000.

Public units (city, county, school district, etc.) receive insurance coverage within a separate category. The official custodian of public unit funds is insured up to $100,000. When the same individual is official custodian for more than one public unit or political subdivision, he is separately insured for the funds held by him for each public unit.

When a public unit establishes a bond redemption account, the investment is deemed to be an investment by a trustee of trust funds. The interests of each bond-holder (as beneficiary) are separately insured up to $100,000. This insurance is separate from the insurance provided for the general funds of the public unit.

The above information is a general summary of FSLIC insurance information. For a complete statement of all rules and regulations, see Title 12, Code of Federal Regulations, Sections 561 and 564.

Receivership Status and the FSLIC-OLD Function

Once the FHLBB has determined that justifiable grounds exist to close a savings association, the Bank Board has the exclusive jurisdiction to appoint the FSLIC as receiver of the failed thrift. Certain considerations apply depending if the thrift holds a state or federal charter. Appointment does not require the involvement of any court. The grounds are as follows: (1) insolvency where the association assets are less than its creditor and member obligations; (2) substantial dissipation of assets or earnings due to any violation of law, rules, or regulations, or any unsafe or unsound practice; (3) an unsafe or unsound condition to transact business; (4) willful violation of a final cease-and-desist order; (5) concealment of association books, papers, records, or assets or refusal to submit the same items to any lawful agent of the Bank Board.

An association placed in FSLIC receivership may contest the FHLBB's action. A suit must be instituted within 30 days in a United States district court praying for an order directing the Bank Board to remove the receiver. If no such action is filed within 30 days, the appointment remains effective until the liquidation process is complete.

The FSLIC as receiver has all the powers, rights, privileges, and responsibilities of a federal association pursuant to federal law. In this capacity, the FSLIC succeeds to all the powers of the association's members, officers, directors, and stockholders. The FSLIC also takes title to the association's assets and without further action succeeds to the association's rights, titles, powers, and privileges. The FSLIC has the power to defend any legal action in which the association has an interest.

The FSLIC is empowered to liquidate a failed association in an orderly manner. Such power to liquidate includes determining the time and manner for asset distribution. Among the important duties of a receiver is to recoup the insurance payments paid by the FSLIC to the many depositors of the failed association. Congress directed the FSLIC to expedite the liquidation process and maintain its insurance reserves. Congress was particularly concerned that protracted delay or failure in the recoupment of insurance payments would have national repercussions.

The FSLIC is not merely the successor to the failed association. In addition to the powers as successor, the receiver is authorized to adjudicate (settle judiciously) the merits and priorities of creditor claims against the failed association. The FSLIC's power to adjudicate the validity of claims became part of the federal regulations nearly thirty years ago. Creditor claims must first be presented to the FSLIC-OLD. The receiver approves any reasonably filed claim proved to its satisfaction. The receiver may wholly or partly disallow any claim of security, preference, or priority. It must notify the claimant of the disallowance and the reason therefor. A disallowed claim may be allowed by the Bank Board. If the claimant is still dissatisfied, he may seek review in federal court.

The Adminstrative Claims Process and Emergency Relief

All claims against a failed association and the receivership estate are transferred from the courts to a federal administrative claims process. These include claims for emergency relief such as temporary restraining orders or temporary injunctions. Two types of procedures for administrative relief are available to claimants: (1) procedures for the administration and determination of expedited relief requests from decisions or threatened actions of the FSLIC as receiver ("Emergency Relief Procedures"), and (2) procedures for the uniform administration and determination of claims filed with the FSLIC as receiver ("Claims Procedures").

Emergency Relief Procedures are typically triggered whenever the receiver threatens to take action against a person or his property, such as posting property for foreclosure because of a loan default or other reason. Experience in the FSLIC receiverships has shown that a debtor faced with foreclosure by the FSLIC will attempt to obtain a temporary restraining order or temporary injunction in court. Debtors will also pursue the administrative remedy afforded by the Emergency Relief Procedures while simultaneously seeking injunctive relief in court. Under *North Mississippi Savings and Loan Association v. Hudspeth,* and 12 U.S.C. 1464(d)(6)(C), the injunction is no longer available to the borrower, but the presumption in Hudspeth was that the affected person would have an administrative remedy available. The emergency relief process provides that remedy.

While threatened foreclosure represents the most visible action by the receiver requiring notice of the available emergency procedures, other situations also present themselves as "threatened action." These generally include: judicial foreclosure, a lawsuit filed by the receiver to collect deficiencies, and the receiver's repudiation of any executory contracts.

Claims Procedures

The administrative claims process is how the receiver deals with all claims against the failed association (which are payable from the receivership estate) that have been dismissed from the courts. It is also used for those claims that have been generated as a result of the receiver's conduct. The outcome of each case will determine each applicant's monetary claim in relation to all other claimants and what remains of the failed thrift's assets being liquidated.

Claims processing is a time consuming affair, which starts with the publication of notice and service of Proof of Claims forms by the receiver. All claims have to be filed within 90 days of first publication.

Under Bank Board procedures, each claim, upon receipt, is analyzed to determine whether it is (1) a routine or "undisputed" claim that will be processed by the FSLIC internally, or (2) a claim that will be referred to the receiver for further investigation and review. Most of the complex claims are referred to the receiver.

The Bank Board procedures include rudimentary discovery rules that are used to complete and verify the evidence submitted with each Proof of Claim form. After the administrative record is designated by the receiver, the receivership Special Representative decides whether the claim is valid, in whole or in part. The claimant can ask that all or certain aspects of the Special Representative's decision be reconsidered. Thereafter, a final determination will be made and mailed to the claimant. If the claimant is dissatisfied, the decision can be appealed to the Bank Board and, if still dissatisfied, the claimant can appeal to the courts.

Much discussion has evolved from the Bank Board's finalization in November 1988 of the *Procedures for the Administration and Determination of Claims Filed with the FSLIC as Receiver.* The purpose of these procedures is to provide for the uniform administration and determination of claims filed with the FSLIC as receiver in all receiverships in the FHLBB System. They are devised to assure compliance with the federal regulations governing the processing and determination of claims. Compliance ensures uniformity of notices to claimants, documentation of claims, determination of the merits of claims by allowance or disallowance in whole or in part, payment of claims, and the review process. Full compliance with these procedures is a prerequisite to FHLBB review. Judicial review of the claim disallowance in whole or in part against the assets of the FSLIC as receiver is available only after exhaustion of these procedures and review and final agency action by the Bank Board.

Coit Independent Joint Venture Vs. FHLBB

In late October 1988, the Supreme Court of the United States heard arguments in the case where a real estate developer, Coit Independent Joint Venture, filed a claim against the Receivership of Firstsouth F.A., Little Rock, Arkansas. The Bank Board obstructed Coit's claim by arguing that the Coit Joint Venture could not seek judicial review until the Bank Board decided whether or not it would pay the claim. The basis of the lawsuit was that Coit contended that it had the right to go to state or federal court without even filing a claim at the receivership level. Coit asserted that the Bank Board had no authority to compel a claimant to undergo an exhaustive review process while the disputed real estate asset wasted away.

In March 1989, the Supreme Court ruled in favor of Coit. Creditors of failed thrifts can contest their claims in court. The high court ruled that Congress did not give the FSLIC initial authority to review disputes between failed thrifts and their creditors.

The Supreme Court's decision will be the crucial determinant in the FSLIC's future administrative claims system. The case highlights the fact that the FSLIC claims process is quite different from the Federal Deposit Insurance Corporation's claim procedures. Failed commercial banks and credit union claimants are free to pursue claims in courts. Justice comments suggest that federal courts rather than the FSLIC should decide claims cases. There appears to be no reason to eliminate claims in state or federal courts despite the necessity for an orderly liquidation process.

Special Representative Delegation

After the FHLBB has delegated the FSLIC as receiver of a failed savings association, a special representative is appointed by the FSLIC-OLD to manage the liquidation of the receivership estate. The special representative with the support of the FHLBB must develop a staff to continue the business of liquidation. Also called a managing officer, the special representative reports directly to a Regional Director of FSLIC.

The primary function of every special representative is the fiduciary responsibility to the creditors of the failed institution. The creditors may include suppliers of goods and professional services prior to the takeover, depositors with accounts exceeding $100,000, former borrowers and debtors, and any other persons with potential claims against the receivership estate. The success of the liquidation effort determines the timeliness and the amount of payment for each claim.

The special representative establishes policies and procedures for the receivership to guide its personnel in the implementation of their responsibilities. He hires, dismisses, and assists in employee evaluations for new job assignments and salary adjustments. The managing officer oversees the existing loan portfolio, delinquent loans, R.E.O. properties, all major construction, ad valorem taxes, and insurance. He monitors the completion of asset business plans and the disposal of assets including any stocks, bonds, personal property, furniture, fixtures, and subsidiary corporations. All legal activity supervision is his direct charge. He interfaces with the Regional Office and receivership controllers in supervising the financial responsibilities of the receivership as well as all financial reporting requirements.

A typical receivership has a local legal counsel firm appointed by the Office of the General Counsel of the FSLIC to handle all the legal complications of a receivership. The managing officer takes charge over this legal contract. In addition, the special representative acts as a liaison between receivership personnel and contract asset managers.

Chapter 6.

THE FSLIC
LIQUIDATION STRATEGY

FSLIC Disposition Objectives

To ensure consistency in the administration of receivership assets, the FSLIC has established policies for asset management, disposition, and the repayment of debt obligations. It is the FSLIC's objective to obtain the highest possible price on a present value basis by using all available options. These include the abilities to restructure troubled debt, temporarily "hold" assets, collect on guarantees and deficiency judgments, and foreclose and sell collateral. The asset management and disposition functions are performed at the lowest cost to the FSLIC in accordance with sound business operations. Problem assets are sold as quickly as is consistent with obtaining the best possible return for the FSLIC or creditors. FSLIC staff and its contractors conduct business in a manner that minimizes costs and maximizes returns.

The goals of the FSLIC's real estate disposition policies encompass a concern for the thrift industry, the general public, and the creditors of failed savings institutions. The FSLIC has a responsibility to maintain the financial integrity of the thrift industry and a fiduciary duty to dispose of assets in an orderly manner for the benefit of the creditors of failed thrifts. Accordingly, the FSLIC attempts to provide for a market driven, rather than a liquidation driven, disposition of controlled assets.

The FSLIC strives to work out and secure a satisfactory repayment of debt obligations, including principal and interest, while seeking a complete and timely liquidation. FSLIC staff evaluate the status of all delinquent loans and pursue strategies for repayment that consider both the maximization of return to the FSLIC and the borrower's financial situation.

The FSLIC may extend relief to borrowers that have exhibited responsible repayment behavior. Types of relief include the restructure of loan terms and payment forbearance for various time periods. Meanwhile, the FSLIC takes necessary steps to maintain asset value and to ensure that its legal rights are preserved. If stronger action is required in seeking repayment, FSLIC staff pursue foreclosure and deficiency judgments against the borrowers or guarantors.

The Business Plan

The primary mechanism used to direct the administration of FSLIC-controlled assets is the asset business plan. The FSLIC requires that business plans be prepared for all material assets. Material assets have a book value at time of acquisition of $500,000 or greater. In developing a business plan, information necessary for prudent management and marketing is collected. The data includes current appraisals, market analyses, and holding cost estimates. FSLIC staff or contractors recommend the most cost-effective management and marketing strategies. Estimated time frames for sales programs strive to provide the highest present value return to the receivership estate without speculating on market fluctuations.

The business plan incorporates an FSLIC appraisal of the property. This value is adjusted on a present value basis for holding and selling costs through closing to arrive at a net realizable value ("NRV"). If the property is an income producing property, a discounted value is computed based upon cost and the time to lease and stabilize the property for a future sale. In this case, the net realizable value represents a value today, for a sale in the future, after stabilization of the property. In addition, an independent receivership evaluation is made of the property. If the evaluation deviates significantly from the appraiser's values, the differences are reconciled.

The Role of Review Committees

To provide essential asset management review and oversight, the FSLIC has established Local and National Review Committees for each FSLIC region. Each committee is composed of skilled professionals having expertise in property management, loan work-outs, mortgage loans, securities, loan servicing, or accounting. The Regional Director, receivership managers, and FSLIC Regional Office staff serve on each committee. These experienced members provide the balance of skills necessary for effective committee deliberations.

The review committees oversee receivership implementation and compliance with applicable federal law, Bank Board regulations, and FSLIC policy. The committees serve as the processing, approving, and monitoring authorities for most large receivership assets. This review and approval procedure provides a means of ensuring that management and marketing efforts are focused on the best disposition strategy for obtaining the highest value for each asset. The review committees serve as each receiver's board of directors to manage and oversee receivership functions.

National Review Committee

National Review Committees meet monthly. Each FSLIC Regional Office (Western, Central, and Eastern) has its own National Committee meeting agenda. Members consist of the Regional Directors, OLD branch chiefs, and the Director of OLD who acts as chairman.

National Review Committees approve asset business plans in excess of $10 million.

Local Review Committees

Local Review Committees are extensions of the FSLIC as Receiver Regional Offices. Depending upon regional needs, meetings are held on an as needed basis, but at least monthly. Local Committees are designed to relieve the workload of the National Review Committees. Local Committees approve business plans of less than $10 million unless the asset is complex in nature. They review and forward business plans over $10 million, as well as Committee activity reports, to the National Review Committee.

Factors Affecting FSLIC Disposition Policy: Hold Vs. Sell

The FSLIC's responsibilities to creditors must be considered in evaluating whether it is a more prudent business decision to hold an asset for future sale or to sell the asset in the current market. A fiduciary relationship exists between the creditors of a failed association and the Federal Savings and Loan Insurance Corporation acting as Receiver. Accordingly, the receiver must manage and liquidate a failed institution in accordance with sound business principles to fulfill its fiduciary responsibilities.

The expression "hold versus sell" implies that only two mutually exclusive strategies exist for the management and liquidation of an asset. There are numerous management strategies with varying time constraints that determine whether an asset is withheld from the marketplace. Each asset has specific needs that must be considered.

The FSLIC does not sell assets until a business plan has been developed and approved. This time period varies, depending on the asset's complexity, availability of reliable information, and expertise required to develop a plan. After approval of a plan, some assets are not offered for sale until committee-approved steps are taken to enhance value. The FSLIC strives to mitigate the financial effect of simultaneously selling a large number of similar FSLIC-controlled properties in a given area. A decision to hold an asset reflects the FSLIC's expectation of a higher present value return for the asset, appropriately discounted for risk. However, the decision to hold a property indefinitely is usually not practical.

For example, a decision to hold and lease a property requires an analysis indicating the market will pay a higher price for an occupied project as opposed to a rundown vacant property. Leasing costs plus a return on tenant finish improvements should accrue to the receivership's creditors in the ultimate sales price. The economic outcome of a leasing scenario requires the market to place a realizable premium on stabilized income-producing assets. However, this higher expected return contains additional risk. Incorrect projections may result in increasing the FSLIC's holding costs, delaying the distribution of cash proceeds to creditors from the asset's sale, and creating an FSLIC cost basis that is impossible to recover.

The Bank Board is concentrating more attention on the traditional "hold versus sell" decisions. Operating cost liability can easily turn a holding decision into a hopeless loss. In disposition, the receiver attempts to retain some of the benefits of increased value added by improved market conditions. In many cases, however, the receiver must provide seller financing to realize a prudent investment return. When the private sector is forced to pay all cash, the FSLIC is hurt since sales proceeds are usually lower. The FSLIC also forfeits the potential for a higher reinvestment yield by not providing term financing to buyers.

The Bank Board's current emphasis has shifted to the disposition of financial institutions. By transferring or merging whole institutions under purchase and assumption transactions, assets remain within the new merged thrifts' portfolios. The assets are not subject to the typical FSLIC liquidation procedures. Those decisions are delegated to others supposedly more familiar with the history and potential of each asset. The Competitive Equality Banking Act of 1987 recognized that regional economies may be temporarily depressed. The asset portfolios of the FSLIC as receiver and other thrifts have suffered severe devaluation in the Southwest and other markets. The FSLIC is frequently retaining a share of each merged institution's future value to ensure some positive return at a much later date.

The FSLIC understands the importance of the nonexistence of private-sector financing for FSLIC asset purchases. However, the FSLIC currently has more pressing issues, and the critical need of FSLIC seller financing remains unattended. Because the mortgage market avoids the inherent risks in FSLIC assets, there is a demand for the type of financing that only the FSLIC can provide. Lack of private financing reduces the number of potential purchasers and inhibits the sale of receivership assets. The financing scarcity increases FSLIC holding costs and promotes lower investment returns.

Dumping

The FSLIC marketing process attempts to maximize value for assets by identifying the optimal disposition strategy for a particular asset through the asset's business plan. Each plan includes a market analysis, a potential buyer assessment, a determination of the asset's strengths and weaknesses, and an evaluation of various selling strategies. This procedural approach precedes the disposition of any asset to assure that value is maximized.

Business plans address whether multiple assets such as condominiums should be sold in a bulk sale or through a retail sales program. Financial scenarios and projected time frames for each alternative are detailed and evaluated. Estimates of the additional transaction and holding costs are considered against the increase in sales revenue and the risk associated with a longer holding period. Market analyses are conducted in the business plan process to identify depressed markets. The detailed analysis of a business plan is necessary to address market supply and demand conditions that relate to various disposition strategies.

Despite the thorough analysis of each business plan, the FSLIC has been accused of "dumping." The concept of dumping as it relates to the sale of assets has several definitions. Dumping is commonly defined as the sale of any asset, or number of assets, that causes a decline in market value of comparable assets in the marketplace. However, dumping also refers to the sale of an asset at a price below book value. This definition does not recognize that it is difficult in a market of declining sales prices, to sell an asset at its historical basis for cash. This meaning also fails to consider that refurbishment funds expended may never add market value to the asset. These connotations have sometimes further contributed to a perception that the FSLIC has been dumping assets.

The variation between the FSLIC's objectives and the disposition goals of financial institutions and private property owners is another contributing factor. An objective of ongoing thrifts is to maintain or increase the net worth of ownership interests. During periods of declining market values, viable businesses are motivated to maintain historical bases in assets to avoid a loss of net worth. However, as receiver, the FSLIC's goal is to maximize the present value of an asset in the marketplace. Receivers are not as concerned about maintaining accounting net worth, as are healthy businesses.

The FSLIC receivership system has taken a practical approach to the sale of receivership assets. Since holding costs greatly decrease final disposition proceeds, the FSLIC strives to spend a minimum on holding costs while extracting the highest sales prices from buyers. Past FSLIC sales history confirms this philosophy.

REO liquidation results for the FSLIC Central Regional Office have averaged 91.55 percent of appraised value since inception. This occurred during a period of decline in the regional real estate market. The FSLIC has been extremely sensitive to market conditions. With a standardized disposition strategy, the FSLIC has maximized the return on REO. Local real estate markets have not been affected negatively.

Chapter 7.

THE FEDERAL ASSET
DISPOSITION ASSOCIATION
(FADA)

The FSLIC's Manpower Shortage

Since 1981 the FSLIC and the FHLBB have handled increasing numbers of failing thrifts without sufficient personnel. Utilizing the authority granted under Section 406 of the National Housing Act, the FSLIC established new federal savings and loan institutions as a means to deal with problem thrifts and conserve the resources of the deposit insurance fund. The FSLIC was not given authority from the Bank Board to hire the employees necessary to manage the anticipated liquidations of failing thrifts. At FSLIC's individual receiverships, where the management, marketing, and disposition occurs, the FSLIC was relying on an extremely small group of nongovernmental employees. While they were charged with a fiduciary responsibility to the institutions' creditors, the FSLIC frequently was their largest creditor.

The Bank Board's failure to provide the FSLIC with additional resources echoed the shortsighted approaches by the Office of Management and Budget (OMB) and the Office of Personnel Management (OPM). Despite the FSLIC's constant reminders that the FSLIC could not perform its statutory responsibilities as receiver, additional staff requests were denied. The FSLIC even suggested that the Reagan administration ratify its policy of reducing unnecessary federal employment by contracting for outside services whenever possible.

As the FSLIC diligently sought to obtain approval from the Bank Board to intensify liquidation forces, San Marino Savings and Loan Association in San Marino, California, with assets just over $800 million failed on December 7, 1984. With FHLBB approval, the FSLIC contracted San Marino's portfolio to a private sector asset management firm. The FSLIC did not have the staff available to manage the assets in-house. The contractor chosen for the assignment was the Victor Palmieri Company, a reputable Los Angeles, California, asset management and disposition firm.

The Bank Board then decided that this was not the appropriate methodology. It severely limited the FSLIC's future use of major contractors to liquidate large portfolios. The FSLIC's authority to hire a significant number of employees to expand its liquidations function was also rescinded. Furthermore, the Bank Board ignored proposals from FSLIC officials who were developing alternatives to assist it in the management, marketing, and disposition of troubled assets acquired from failed institutions.

Alternatives to Assist The FSLIC's Liquidation Efforts

During the period from 1983 through 1985, the FSLIC's Directors presented the Bank Board with alternatives for dealing with the increasing caseload of troubled savings and loan institutions. The alternatives included the following:

1. The Bank Board could approve the present system which allows the hiring of nonfederal employees. That program decreased the need for hundreds of additional federal employees.

2. The Bank Board could adopt a liquidations system similar to the Federal Deposit Insurance Corporation's (FDIC), which might require: a) a statutory change since the FSLIC's governing statutes are different from the FDIC's, and b) the approval of the Office of Personnel Management (OPM) and the Office of Management and Budget (OMB) to hire career federal employees and lower grade liquidation staff.

3. The FSLIC could develop special purpose contracts which would allow the FSLIC to selectively contract with individuals to serve as quasi-federal employees or independent contractors for the purpose of engaging their services for decentralized services under the supervision of the FSLIC liquidation staff.

4. The FSLIC could expand the use of contracting which would allow FSLIC receiverships to enter into broader contracts for general management services and specific functional services.

5. The Bank Board could establish an Office of Liquidations within the Federal Home Loan Bank System, with reporting responsibility to the Bank Board through the FSLIC Director. While this office would be associated with the FSLIC, it would have enhanced flexibility to hire and compensate employees as necessary. (The Office of Liquidations would be similar to the establishment of the Bank Board's Office of Finance and the Office of Regulatory Policy, Oversight, and Supervision. Both Offices operate within the Bank System. Since the Office directors report directly to the Bank Board, the Bank Board has minimized added layers of bureaucracy.)

6. The Bank Board could delegate the Office of Liquidations as an FSLIC agent under the Federal Home Loan Bank System. This would allow receivership employees to become Bank System employees funded through their receiverships.

7. The Bank Board could obtain legislation to form a federal asset management corporation. The corporate entity would copy the structure of the Federal Home Loan Mortgage Corporation, which would serve as the FSLIC's liquidation agent. The corporation would operate as a profit-making, industry-owned corporation with the Bank Board members as its board of directors. The FSLIC's Operations and Liquidations Division would then become part of the management corporation. It would manage the liquidation of FSLIC and receivership assets for a management fee and a share of the proceeds.

In addition to these alternatives, the FSLIC recommended that the OPM deliver an opinion on whether the work of receivership employees was so "governmental" that it had to be performed by federal employees. The FSLIC requested the opinion in light of the various changes in law since 1942. Recent modification of federal policy supported contracting services when practical. The FSLIC assumed the OPM's position would be that receivership work was not intrinsically "governmental."

It is not clear whether the OMB ever officially granted approval. Requests to fill 94 FSLIC vacancies in 1986 and another 74 FSLIC vacancies in 1987 were denied. Meanwhile, the Bank Board proposed a hiring freeze, and thus the FSLIC was again denied staff increases.

An ambivalent commitment on the part of the Bank Board to the receivership system impeded its development. The Bank Board was consistently perceived to be unaware or uninterested in the receivership system. The Bank Board never addressed questions regarding the legality of the receivership system which were raised by the Office of General Counsel on numerous occasions. The Bank Board's attitude towards the receivership system created an atmosphere of uncertainty and a fear of imminent dismantling.

The Bank Board was presented with seven alternatives to address the FSLIC's liquidation needs. These included options to enhance its functions by expanding in-house resources and establishing a new office to support its liquidation efforts. Despite these suggestions, the Bank Board decided to create a private entity to perform this important government function. The decision came as a complete surprise to many observers.

The Thrift Industry Solution
The Bank Board's failure to address the manpower problem internally presented the perfect opportunity for the Federal Savings and Loan Advisory Council (FSLAC) and the United States League of Savings Institutions to resolve the problem. During the summer of 1985, the FSLAC developed the concept of a "406" association to be created under the National Housing Act. Although the Management Consignment Program would still remain active, this newly created entity would incorporate the skills and expertise of the private sector. The industry, through the FSLAC, conveyed the private entity concept as an advantage to the FSLIC. The FSLIC could utilize the private group to provide interim management and asset liquidation in troubled institutions with the Bank Board's

approval. Through the industry's broad interpretation of Sections 406(a), (b), and (c) of the National Housing Act of 1934 and its influence over the Bank Board, the Bank Board sanctioned the creation of the Federal Asset Disposition Association (FADA). Thus, the FADA was not created by or pursuant to specific congressional legislation.

What Is the FADA?

The Federal Asset Disposition Association(FADA) was chartered as a federal savings and loan association by the Federal Home Loan Bank Board on November 5, 1985. The FADA is wholly owned by the FSLIC. The association's home office was to be Denver, Colorado. Duration of the association was granted for a ten year period. The association's objectives were the acquisition, acceptance, orderly liquidation, and disposition of assets acquired by the FSLIC in its role as receiver. As agent serving on behalf of receivers, the FADA did not take title to underlying assets but did have fiduciary responsibilities inherent in the agency function.

Upon the FADA's creation, the Bank Board appointed eleven voting directors and three nonvoting directors as board members of the agency. The three nonvoting members were to serve for one year with possible reappointment. They included the Director of the FSLIC, the FADA's president, and one president from the Bank Board system. While the FSLIC Director represented the FSLIC on the FADA board, the FSLIC maintained no voting power on the FADA Board of Directors even though the FSLIC owned 100 percent of the FADA's stock.

The Bank Board also assisted in the capitalization of the FADA. To secure the financial base of the FADA, the FSLIC provided the FADA with capital for start-up costs and general operations. By 1986 the Bank Board had purchased 25,000 shares of stock, thus capitalizing the FADA with $25 million. The FSLIC also authorized a $200 million line of credit for the FADA backed by a contract between the FSLIC and the Federal Home Loan Bank of Topeka. The FADA had a guaranteed repayment of up to $50 million of advances from the FSLIC. The repayment guarantee applied only to advances used for the purpose of funding operations in which the

FADA had a legal agreement with the FSLIC as receiver or conservator for an insured institution. Interest was charged to the FADA on outstanding draws at the FHLB cost of funds rate.

The new agency was never designed to operate as a savings and loan institution. The FADA, however, could accept funds for deposit with express consent of the Board. Per the NHA Sections 407(a) and (b), asset liquidation and interim management were its primary objectives. The agency recruited private sector professionals with liberal compensation packages. Salaries and benefits exceeded those paid to Federal government employees. The agency was encouraged to utilize real estate management resources other than its own regional personnel in assisting the FSLIC with its diverse geographic distribution of assets. The FSLIC was required to transfer its assets to the new agency at liquidation value.

Early FADA Objectives

The FADA, as envisioned in its early stages by the FSLIC's senior officials, was to consist of 50 to 80 real estate experts who would provide cost effective solutions to the FSLIC's burgeoning asset caseload. The general mission of this group was to enhance the FSLIC's asset management and disposition functions through its real estate expertise. The FADA engaged in three types of contractual agreements: (1) an asset management agreement with the FSLIC as receiver, (2) an asset advisory agreement with Management Consignment Program institutions or other financially troubled institutions with the FSLIC's approval, and (3) an agreement with the FSLIC to provide advisory/consulting services. The FADA's objective was to obtain the best return to the FSLIC on a net present value basis. Its goal was to devise flexible, creative solutions for problem assets which typically defy traditional methods of asset management.

The FADA's disposition function was twofold: presenting strategies or recommendations regarding the disposal of assets and marketing those assets. The agency disposed of assets either through the workout of nonperforming loans or through the sale of properties.

The FADA Becomes an Autonomous Agency

The FADA was instituted solely to provide assistance to the FSLIC, who is its only stockholder. However, the line of ultimate authority became diffused. When the FADA was organized, the Bank Board created a problem by establishing a separate board of directors for the FADA. This board of directors assumed total control of the FADA. It created a management system whereby executives would take direction only from the FADA board. Problems resulted when the FADA provided direct assistance to the FSLIC but received overall guidance from its own board of directors. The Bank Board did not correct this chain of command weakness. Therefore, the FSLIC was severely hampered in exercising its authority over the FADA.

This diffused line of authority produced a multitude of problems. The issues included the FADA's evolvement into a large bureaucratic entity and the development of policies and procedures separate from the standard Federal government regulations. Other concerns involved the employment of staff who maintained active interests in real estate investment and development companies with ties to the savings and loan industry. The FADA's view of itself as independent from the FSLIC resulted in problems concerning cooperation, communication, and fiduciary responsibility.

The FADA perpetuated this autonomous view by developing its own business code of ethics in lieu of federal practices. With the aid of private consultants, the FADA developed its own code of conduct. Certain ties to the thrift industry were not appropriate for government employees with similar duties. As agent for the FSLIC receiverships, the FADA had accompanying fiduciary responsibilities to the creditors. The FADA should have adhered to the same conflict of interest policies and procedures which FSLIC/Bank Board employees and their subcontractors followed.

The FADA Refused to Acknowledge the FSLIC

The FADA's accountability to the FSLIC was unclear from its very beginning. The FADA believed it was a separate corporation subject to the supervision of its board of directors. The FADA's board members and senior staff felt it was unnecessary to bring matters to the attention of the FSLIC. The FSLIC Operations and Liquidations Division (OLD) by law was empowered with authority over contractors. However, the OLD found it very challenging to exert its authority over the FADA. This was due to the vague definition of the relationship. While the OLD could hire and fire other private contractors, the FSLIC-OLD could not fire the FADA. The FADA was not an OLD in the hierarchy that extends from the Bank Board. The FADA continued to operate as an independent bureaucracy reporting to its board of directors.

The FADA relieved itself of accountability to the FSLIC and operated as an independent entity by establishing a separate bureaucracy. This tendency to view itself as independent of the FSLIC was the driving force behind its lack of communication with FSLIC receiverships. Another considerable reason for the communication hiatus stemmed from a combination of the Bank Board's failure and the FSLIC's inability to define a clear relationship between the FSLIC and the FADA. Despite the FADA's lack of authority, the FADA insisted on controlling asset litigation, even though the FSLIC retained asset litigation experts acutely aware of FSLIC's "receivership superpowers" regarding the latest legal cases and regulatory authority governing the FSLIC. Several attempts were made by FSLIC senior managers to rectify the situation. These attempts were countered by the FADA's implicit efforts to exert independence.

Ironically, the assumed power of the FADA stemmed from the asset management contract each receivership executed to employ the FADA. That contract provided FADA employees with a limited power of attorney. It did not allow the FADA to assume all of the FSLIC's receivership powers, such as rescinding contracts, defending lawsuits, or adjudicating creditor claims. The Bank Board prolonged the authority controversy by giving all new receivership asset management contracts exclusively to the FADA.

A Conflict of Sales Strategies—the FADA Vs. the FSLIC

The FADA initially disposed of assets through the workout of nonperforming loans or through the sale of properties. However, the FADA did not follow the same disposition philosophy as the

FSLIC. The FADA's objective was to thoroughly negotiate with troubled borrowers. This placed assets in a prolonged holding pattern, while the FADA collected management fees. The FADA spent an inordinate amount of time trying to restructure loans. In the past that practice proved extremely costly and time consuming by doing little to replenish the FSLIC's deposit insurance fund. The fiduciary responsibility belonged to the creditors, not to the borrowers. Ultimately taxpayers funded the costs for lengthy restructuring negotiations.

The FADA was proud of its expertise in restructuring non-performing loans. As of January 1, 1988, the FADA claimed that almost 47 percent of its total disposition activities were in the restructuring of loans and that hundreds of millions of dollars worth were in the pipeline. These figures were unsettling since renegotiated loans did little to recover proceeds for FSLIC. According to FSLIC officials, "restructured debt was the worst option available; it did not provide liquidity and did not collect the delinquent debt because the majority of loans defaulted again. Restructured debt could never be of better quality than the real estate since it is one step removed from title to the real estate." In view of the FSLIC's position, FADA officials should not have spent a significant amount of time restructuring delinquent debt. Instead, the FADA should have worked to obtain title to the real estate. The FADA's stance favoring restructuring directly contradicted FSLIC disposition policy. Yet FADA continued to collect fees through the debt restructuring process. What private sector business would have continued to pay an agent who consistently refused to follow instructions?

The FADA Became the FSLIC's Exclusive Contractor

Since the FADA's inception, numerous contractors that provided management services to the FSLIC were replaced by the FADA. Many reputable contractors felt there was an inherent bias against the selection of firms that had previously done work for the FSLIC. It was the view of the private sector contractors that the FADA excluded experienced and highly qualified firms for political reasons.

During mid-1986 and early 1987, the FADA regularly told the Bank Board that it was having problems with the FSLIC. Receiverships did not rely solely on the FADA for asset management and advisory contracts. Several directives were sent to receivership managing officers to enter into contracts with the FADA to manage troubled assets.

These directives were not received warmly by the FSLIC receiverships. They were just beginning to become familiar with the FADA's capabilities and performance. Before long, FSLIC receiverships' complaints about the FADA's operational performance filtered back to the Bank Board. The Bank Board was seriously concerned that the FSLIC and the FADA would never work together.

As a result, the Bank Board's Chief of Staff made field visits to FSLIC receiverships to determine the reason for the lack of compliance with the stated directives. Soon after these visits were made, the Bank Board established the FSLIC Restructuring Task Force.

The Bank Board charged FSLIC's Restructuring Task Force with two goals: to assure effectiveness and cost efficiency in the management and disposition of FSLIC assets and to ascertain which functions would be transferred to the FADA. The use of the Task Force attempted to satisfy the FADA board of directors' demand to use only the FADA for asset management. The Task Force did not acknowledge the FSLIC's authority over the FADA. It did confirm the FSLIC's responsibility to evaluate the performance of its current subcontractors and if deemed unacceptable to transfer the assets under their control to the FADA.

Not long after the Task Force's report was released, the FSLIC's Director, issued a new policy directive on March 26, 1987. The directive insisted that the FADA be given every opportunity to provide asset management until its resource limitations were strained. FSLIC staff were required to reevaluate their portfolios in an effort to assign more assets to the FADA. The Bank Board's actions clearly reflected the influence of the FADA board of directors. In spite of the numerous and serious concerns raised throughout the FSLIC receivership system, the Bank Board seemed committed to guaranteeing FADA's existence and expansion.

An Overview of FADA Activities

On January 31, 1986, the FADA filed with the FHLBB its *Proposed Strategy and Operations,* constituting its business plan. The 1986 business plan provided the FADA's mission statement, purpose, and operational strategy. On February 1, 1986, Roslyn B. Payne was selected by the FADA board of directors as President and Chief Executive Officer. Basic legal documentation consisting of contracts between the FSLIC as receiver or conservator and the FADA for asset management and disposition services was completed in July 1986. A standard contract for work with the FSLIC in its corporate capacity was executed in October 1986. At that time, the FADA acted as the FSLIC's agent for services in three ways: (1) an asset management and disposition agreement with the FSLIC as receiver, (2) an asset advisory agreement with Management Consignment Program (MCP) institutions or other financially troubled institutions with the FSLIC's consent, and (3) an agreement with the FSLIC in its corporate capacity. The FADA was engaged for its first asset management and disposition assignment on July 18, 1986, with the FSLIC as receiver for Sun Savings and Loan Association, San Diego, California. On October 31, 1986, the FADA employed 128 professionals. As of February 27, 1987, the FADA had a staff of 199 and had established its administrative offices in San Francisco. Four key offices had been located in Denver, Atlanta, Dallas, and Los Angeles. Temporary offices had also been established in West Palm Beach, Houston, and Washington to help with FSLIC engagements. By January 1, 1988, the staff of real estate experts had mushroomed to over 400.

What Were the Problems?

Lackadaiscal Attitude

The FADA's laxness in contract asset management responsibilities resulted in financial losses to the receiverships. The FADA billed receiverships full asset management fees while FSLIC receivership personnel actually performed many of the FADA's asset management duties. Receivership staff believed it was necessary to assume the FADA's duties because the FADA failed to fulfill basic management tasks.

Fiduciary Disrespect

The FSLIC's fiduciary responsibility to creditors is a very serious facet of the receiver's duties. Creditors are individual depositors, vendors, or contractors which have valid payment claims against a failed thrift. Creditors are paid money from liquidating assets of failed institutions. According to the FSLIC, a fiduciary is someone who is entrusted with the care of another person's money, property, or other items of value. Thus, an abridgement of such responsibility arose due to the FADA's negligence.

Late Business Plans

The FSLIC requires its asset managers (including the FADA) to produce preliminary business plans and final business plans within 30 and 90 days, respectively, after receipt of the asset. Business plans provide summaries on the background, management, and future strategies of disposing of an asset. The FADA consistently submitted its business plans late and incomplete.

The preliminary business plan provides a "snapshot" look at an asset as of the date of closure. It also contains brief preliminary recommendations on managing and disposing of the asset. The final business plan analyzes the asset and recommends the management and disposition strategy that delivers the highest return to the FSLIC. After the plans are submitted, the managing officer of the receivership can approve plans under $500,000. Plans over $500,000 are approved by a Local Review Committee; plans in excess of $10 million are approved at the National Review Committee meetings. At both the Local and National Review Committee meetings, receivership and FADA personnel, along with the contractors responsible for producing the plans, are required to present their plans and answer questions asked by FSLIC senior management.

Without these plans, the receiver had no effective control of an asset. It was unable to: (1) assess its borrowing requirements, (2) accurately project repayment of loans by the FSLIC, (3) estimate liquidating dividends for creditor distribution, and (4) ascertain if the FADA was effectively managing its assets. The FADA, in many cases, subcontracted the preparation of preliminary and final business plans. The FADA's reliance on contracting services resulted in minimal subcontractor oversight, untrained subcontractors, and insufficient quality control. The practice of contracting for services caused double payments for the same work. Payments were made to the FADA as asset manager, and to the subcontractor who actually performed the work. The FSLIC could have contracted directly with the subcontractor and avoided the FADA's fees. The FSLIC was obligated for payment since the FADA could pass through all costs incurred. This procedure contrasted sharply with private asset management firms retained by the FSLIC. These firms prepared their own business plans as part of their asset management fees.

Insurance Oversights

The FADA not only exhibited questionable management of assets through untimely and poor quality business plans but also (1) neglected to secure properties, which resulted in financial losses and potential liability claims for receiverships; (2) failed to inform the FSLIC of property insurance claims until the FSLIC made repeated requests, which in several instances resulted in the receiverships carrying assets without insurance coverage; and (3) incurred excessive insurance premiums and taxes to protect assets in which receiverships had potentially no equity. Violations of FSLIC liquidation procedures caused receiverships to incur insurance losses and jeopardized the insurance coverage of other receivership assets.

Marketing Deficiencies

Marketing brochures initially developed by the FADA also caused conflict. Specific information such as net operating income, sales prices, and locational maps were missing. A copyright notice and disclaimer were included to prevent sales information inconsistency. Brokers complained since they could not reproduce the vague data for potential buyers. Although the FADA's advertising approach left much to be desired, potential purchasers somehow found out about the assets and called to make inquiries. The FADA handled these calls poorly. Some individuals were told that information requests must be submitted in writing to San Francisco headquarters. Others were told that the FADA did not have properties for sale and that the FADA only managed FSLIC properties.

Determined individuals who did call the San Francisco office were told to continue calling because the FADA would like to get to know them. However, in order to receive property information, the caller would have to submit a questionnaire, an outline of recent acquisitions, a financial profile, and a letter from a potential lending institution. These procedures were unrealistic since most of FADA's properties initially were only available for sale on a cash basis. Thus, a financial statement and lender information were unnecessary. This cumbersome process acted as a deterrent for seriously interested buyers. Brokers refused to complete the questionnaires, especially to name their buyers.

Excessive Personnel Costs

The FADA's high overhead costs, particularly salaries and related compensation, fostered the potential for diminishing returns to the FSLIC. Roslyn Payne, former FADA President and Chief Executive Officer, earned an annual salary of $250,000. In 1986 the top 17 officials were paid annual combined salaries of $2.1 million. At a time when FADA had not yet developed performance criteria, these same officials received additional performance bonuses of nearly $200,000 for six months or less of work. Ms. Payne received the highest bonus at $75,000. Despite a steady decline in its capital, the FADA awarded salary increases to its senior executives ranging between 4 and 10 percent. Later, after extensive controversy, Roslyn Payne resigned. Many executive staff members left the FADA. Replacement salaries averaged considerably less thereafter.

Extraordinary Travel and Telephone Expenses

During its first 18 months of operation, the FADA spent $1.8 million for its own administrative travel. This was in addition to travel for asset management which the FADA charged the FSLIC. The FADA incurred nearly $950,000 for telephone expenses, including the use of auto and airplane phones. FADA executives gave frequent presentations to lobbying groups and met frequently with members of Congress, state savings and loan leagues, representatives from savings and loan institutions, and newspaper and television reporters.

Meal and hotel costs for FADA executives were high since FADA staff were not bound by Federal government travel regulations. These rules restricted luxuries such as laundry service, spousal travel, and excessive dinner bills with no documentation. A per diem schedule was generally enforced for government employees.

Huge Occupancy Costs

In the same 18 month period, the FADA's occupancy expenses totaled $2.2 million. These were also expensed to the FSLIC. This may not be excessive for a private sector entity, but it appeared high for an organization responsible for recovering funds for depositors and creditors.

The FADA's charter stated its headquarters was to be located in Denver, Colorado. After Roslyn Payne accepted the position as CEO, the administrative headquarters was moved to San Francisco near Ms. Payne's home. The FADA chose not to maintain office space in buildings owned by receiverships. Instead, it leased office space in high rent districts from the private sector. For example, FADA's San Francisco headquarters, with its breathtaking view of the Golden Gate Bridge, cost over $66,000 per month. The FADA claimed this was sublet space obtained at a reduced rate.

In addition, FADA's Dallas office negotiated a five year irrevocable lease for office space with monthly rental payments of nearly $42,000. The FADA could have occupied any number of FSLIC-controlled properties. Providing no further expansion of its Dallas office space, the FADA's total rental obligation for this space exceeds $2 million through July 1992.

Burdensome Equipment Rental Expenses

During its first 18 months of operation, the FADA incurred equipment expenses of $2.3 million which were charged to the FSLIC. A significant portion of this expense was related to the FADA's development of an extensive management information system (MIS). Without consulting the FSLIC, the FADA entered into an irrevocable lease for computer equipment, which FSLIC officials identified as incompatible with FSLIC's asset management reporting system. The incompatibility of the FADA and FSLIC computer systems was brought to the attention of the responsible individuals, who established the FSLIC Management Information Systems (MIS) Task Force to resolve the issue. However, FADA did not attend any meetings, nor did it assign a representative to sit on the task force.

The Bottom Line . . .
The FADA's Initial Services Were Too Expensive

In carrying out its work for FSLIC, the FADA's so-called "private-sector expertise" did not necessarily come from the FADA, but rather from subcontractors who performed those services for the FADA. The FADA's parceling out of its work resulted in FSLIC receiverships assuming increased costs and unnecessary responsibility for the oversight of quality control in FADA subcontractors' work.

In reality, a major portion of the FADA's work, including preliminary and final business plans, was performed by subcontractors. The FSLIC also used subcontractors for a large part of its asset management and disposition work. The FSLIC endorsed the use of the FADA primarily because it would provide the FSLIC with real estate expertise not found within its own organization or among the numerous subcontractors previously used by the FSLIC. Yet when the FADA sprang into full operation in July 1986, it began drawing on a pool of subcontractors, many of whom the FSLIC had already dealt with, to provide the FSLIC with the expertise which it had initially hoped the FADA would provide.

The FADA's employment of subcontractors to perform a significant amount of receivership work limited the FADA from meeting optimum cost and efficiency goals. FSLIC receivers could perform more efficiently by subcontracting work in-house to major asset management/disposition companies that had performed successfully for the FSLIC in the past.

The FADA's Accountability to the FSLIC Remains Unclear

The FADA's accountability to the FSLIC remains unclear. Specifically, the FADA believes that it is a separate corporation subject to the control and direction of its board of directors. The FADA's president and chairman of the board have repeatedly raised policy issues and difficulties directly with Bank Board members. These problems should have been brought to the attention of the FSLIC Director or other senior FSLIC officials for resolution. A FADA board member expressed the opinion that although FSLIC staff wanted the FADA to be supervised by the Operations and Liquidations Division, such supervision was not proper. Within documents analyzing FSLIC concerns, the FADA expressed that it must retain the right to bring matters directly to the Board.

According to the FSLIC's Office of the General Counsel (OGC), the Operations and Liquidations Division has authority over contractors the FSLIC utilizes in the liquidation of failed institutions. The OGC has stated that the FSLIC must maintain its responsibility and accountability for contractors and for the manner in which these contractors carry out functions delegated to them. The FSLIC must be able to provide assurances that all receiverships and supporting contracted services are carried out in the most efficient, effective, and economical manner, in accordance with policies and procedures, legal/regulatory requirements, and contract terms.

While the FSLIC seems to have been given authority over contractors, FSLIC management has found it very challenging to exert such authority over the FADA due to the lack of a definition of the relationship between the FSLIC and the FADA. To illustrate the FSLIC's concerns and frustration in exerting its authority over the FADA, FSLIC's Deputy Director stated in a memorandum during October 1986 to FSLIC's Director that: "The FSLIC and the OLD badly need help for complex workouts and formulating business plans for large or impaired real estate. The OLD Director and his organization are under the direct control of the Director of the FSLIC. The FSLIC can hire and fire within this group as necessary to insure proper accountability. The same cannot be said for the FSLIC's relationship with the FADA. The FADA is not and never will be an OLD in the hierarchy that extends from the Bank Board. The OLD wears the government mantle. The FADA is a subsidiary— a semi-private operation—a broker/contractor. The FADA is not Uncle Sam. Uncle Sam is supposed to control the FADA."

The FADA Dissolution Act

In October 1988, during the closing hours of the 100th Congress, the House of Representatives voted for the second time to pass the FADA Dissolution Act. As with the first vote, a necessary two-thirds majority could not be attained. The bill required the Bank Board to dispose of the FADA's charter within 60 days of the measure's passage. The dissolution could have involved several alternatives. However, the Bank Board would not have been able to sell the FADA as an operating company if it were dissolved.

In September 1988 the FADA sale proposal was tendered by the then current head of the FADA, Gerald P. Carmen. Tired of the constant barrage of complaints waged against the FADA, Carmen recommended to FHLBB Chairman Danny Wall the sale of the FADA to private industry. The proposal stated that FADA's receivership asset management contracts could possibly be worth millions of dollars if they were offered for sale. Carmen's suggestion was made in response to numerous FADA, thrift industry, and Congressional Budget Office statements arguing that FADA's dissolution would cause countless delays and huge losses for the FSLIC. Short of an outright sale, Carmen also advised the merging of the remaining FADA personnel into the FSLIC liquidation operation.

The FADA issue will always draw intense debate. It is unlikely that Congress will allow a sale of the FADA to private industry. It seems logical that the FADA and the FSLIC should be merged into the FDIC Division of Liquidation. The FSLIC, the OLD, the FDIC, and the FADA as one force should control the management and disposition of failed thrift assets. As the REO volume increases, private sector subcontractors must assume more responsibility in the management and liquidation of these assets. The FSLIC, the FADA, and the FDIC combined do not have the necessary resources to complete the resolution of the savings and loan crisis. A partnership between the public and private sectors is the sensible answer.

Chapter 8.

HOW THE FSLIC
REALLY SELLS ASSETS

FSLIC Policy and Procedure

As the total of failed thrift assets escalated into the billions of dollars, the FSLIC placed greater emphasis upon accountability for the management and disposition of assets. The FSLIC frequently acted in the capacities of thrift industry promoter, congressionally authorized insurer of savings accounts, and liquidator of failed thrift assets. The potential for conflicts of interest grew as insolvencies increased. In the early 1980s the FSLIC through its Operations and Liquidations Division (OLD) developed and implemented rigid policies and procedures to ensure the responsible yet timely sale of assets. These procedures provide a framework for disposing of assets at market value. They ensure the effective oversight and accountability of the liquidation process.

Appraisals

The first activity in the liquidation of FSLIC assets is the ordering of a new appraisal. Although existing appraisals on file at closed institutions are reviewed for accuracy and conformance with applicable standards, rarely are these existing appraisals adopted by the FSLIC.

Appraisal procurement for FSLIC receivership properties is co-ordinated by FSLIC staff. The valuation of FSLIC receivership properties by appraisers has a significant impact on the management and marketing of an asset. Unbiased appraisals serve as a crucial underpinning of proper asset management. The FSLIC strives to ensure that no undue influence is exerted over any appraiser.

FSLIC receivership appraisals generally conform to the FHLBB Memorandum R-41C. The R-41C standards are applied to all properties. Market value is based upon the following:

The most probable price that a property should bring in a competitive and open market under all conditions requisite to a fair sale. The buyer and seller each act prudently and knowledgeably. The price is not affected by undue stimulus. This definition assumes the sale closes on a specified date and the title transfers from seller to buyer under certain conditions:

1. buyer and seller are typically motivated;

2. both parties are well informed, and each is acting in his own best interest;

3. a reasonable time is allowed for exposure in the open market;

4. payment is made in cash or its equivalent; and

5. the price represents the normal consideration for the property sold. Special financing or sales concessions are not utilized.

Market value is not intended to be a fire-sale liquidation value for receivership properties.

The appraisal must employ the following recognized appraisal methods and techniques:

Cost approach

The cost approach includes proper adjustments for any items detrimental to stability or marketability, such as physical and functional depreciation or economic obsolescence. The estimated land value indicates the market value of the land, recognizing its highest and best use.

Market approach

The value indicated by the market approach is supported by any analysis of sales of at least three comparable properties, preferably located close to the subject premises and recently sold. The appraiser reports and analyzes any prior sales of the subject property within the last three years.

Income approach

The value indicated by the income approach is derived from the following economic factors:

1. The forecasted gross income is based on rents or leases, currently obtained from comparable buildings similar in amenities, location, size, style, and quality.

2. The estimated expenses, including replacement reserves, are comparable with known and verified local expenses. Estimated expenses also reflect any increases in taxes, utilities, and other operating costs.

3. The estimated vacancy loss rates are supported with historical and current experience in the mortgaged premises' locale.

4. The capitalization rate reflects the overall demands of knowledgeable investors for the property type on the appraisal date.

5. The gross rent multiplier is derived from recent sales of comparable local properties. It is properly adjusted for the overall quality and reliability of the gross income the property can be expected to produce.

Receipt of the appraisal report marks the end of a long waiting period. The time from initial written purchase order to delivery of the physical appraisal report averages six to eight weeks, with three months or longer possible for sizeable commercial projects. Because of past appraisal controversies and subsequent federal guideline modifications, appraisers are extremely careful to author a professionally correct product. That caution creates time delays, especially when an individual receivership must order hundreds of appraisals. Another obstacle is the fact that appraisers who had appraisal work in the files of closed institutions usually are not contacted for any new appraisals. The FSLIC effort to minimize any possible conflict of interest is apparent.

FSLIC-approved appraisers maintain senior membership in national appraisal organizations. The FSLIC requires the appraiser to have five years of cumulative appraisal experience (primarily with nonresidential property in a specialized field), an excellent professional reputation, and the ability to render accurate and unbiased value opinions. FSLIC appraisers possess the analytical ability and mature judgment to discern trends and economic value influences. Their final narrative reports must include the rationale for value conclusions.

Each appraisal contains a justification for the suggested marketing period and discount rate, estimated construction or lease-up completion dates, and the valuation methods used. The appraisal is made in accordance with guidelines established by the FSLIC Executive Director.

Upon receipt, the appraisal report is reviewed and analyzed. After the appraisal is judged satisfactory, information about market value, highest and best use, and absorption is incorporated into the business plan. Future income projections are modified as required by the appraisal. Incomplete projects generally are appraised at the "as is" or "as completed" value.

Net Realizable Value (NRV)

An asset manager must prepare a net realizable value (NRV) analysis of each asset based on the new appraisal. The NRV is a measure of the present value of the net cash proceeds to be realized from the disposition of an asset, adjusted for the costs associated with holding the asset and closing the sale. Specifically, the NRV is calculated by adjusting the appraised value for direct selling costs, holding costs, operating income (if applicable), costs to improve or complete the property, litigation costs, and contractor fees. An NRV worksheet is prepared for each viable management and disposition strategy. The NRV is updated and reviewed annually.

The NRV is the benchmark for cash proceeds the receiver should obtain upon the sale of an asset. Although each receivership always strives to sell for as close to what the market will bear, that concept is not always possible. Frequently new appraisals recommend asset sales at a later point in time. When an asset cannot be sold quickly for market value, the receiver must expend significant dollars to maintain and operate the property. Expenditures for maintenance and repair, security, taxes, and insurance are common to all assets. An asset manager should be able to discount the price to sell an asset quicker. The shorter holding period results in less operating costs expended and an overall greater return for the FSLIC.

Business Plans Are Critical

An asset manager must prepare a business plan for each material asset (an asset having a book value of $500,000 or more at the time that the FSLIC acquires control of such asset). Business plans function as the primary tools for managing and controlling the asset liquidation process. The requirement to prepare business plans extends to FADA asset management contractors as well as to FSLIC receivership and corporate staff. Nonmaterial assets are managed and liquidated in accordance with the same guidelines for larger real estate assets.

Immediately following the acquisition of an asset, the asset manager prepares a preliminary business plan. Critical information from existing files and records is compiled into the plan to enable the asset manager to make appropriate business decisions on time sensitive issues. This plan provides the basis for interim asset management until the final business plan is completed and approved.

The preliminary business plan includes an estimate of the asset's net realizable value (NRV), which is submitted to the appropriate review committee for approval pending the receipt of the new appraisal report. Once the estimated NRV is established, the asset manager and FSLIC staff address problems to clear title, resolve loan participation squabbles, and determine whether to cancel contractual obligations, including construction loans in progress and takeout commitments. Efforts are directed to urgent issues, such as encumbrances, pending construction loan draws, canceled casualty or liability insurance, income collection, and collateral deterioration.

Asset managers update and augment the preliminary business plans and present the revised final business plans to the appropriate review committees for approval. The final business plan becomes the strategic plan for an asset's management and disposition. Each plan addresses unique asset characteristics by evaluating market conditions, specific operational data, legal issues, and economic alternatives for assessing value. In developing the plan, the asset manager considers and evaluates all practical management and liquidation strategies, and recommends the strategy that maximizes the asset's value. The asset manager assesses the financial feasibility of viable alternative disposition strategies, performs a net realizable value (NRV) analysis, and establishes minimum sales prices.

Review Committees

The business plan approval process ensures that all appropriate management and disposition strategies are evaluated and that the optimal strategy for maximizing asset value is pursued. The Local and National Review Committees are composed of individuals possessing the skills necessary to provide the objective deliberation needed to approve, disapprove, or amend business plans.

Committee members can be compared to the senior loan committee review members in a large bank. Members are not bashful in ferreting out potential problems. Oftentimes plans are tabled until requested information is obtained. Business plans that are rejected by the review committees are revised and resubmitted. Asset managers submit semiannual reports to the appropriate level of delegated authority regarding the status of business plan implementation. In addition to the business plan approval process, the review committees review and oversee business plan implementation and evaluate the performance of asset managers.

Any major deviation from an approved final business plan must be sanctioned by the appropriate review committee. First the change must be approved by the Local Review Committee and then ratified by the National Review Committee. An example of a major change is the sale of any asset for less than 90 percent of appraised value. Approval of a term contract that extends FSLIC financing requires additional committee approval.

Types of Real Estate Assets Available

The original responsibility of thrift institutions was to make home mortgage loans. Congress changed that with the Garn-St Germain Act of 1982. From 1982 through 1985, Congress allowed the thrifts to invest in all types of commercial ventures. Once the FHLBB relaxed accounting rules and capital requirements, the savings and loan industry proceeded to make loans and take equity positions in everything from office buildings to recreational time shares. Therefore, the variety of FSLIC receivership portfolio assets is extremely diverse.

FSLIC receivership assets are found in numerous ownership forms. Thrift assets include residential mortgages, commercial loans, loan participations with other financial institutions, joint ventures with developers, and outright ownership through subsidiary corporations, to name only a few. Subsequent foreclosures caused by mortgage defaults result in the ownership of a myriad of different kinds of real estate. These include raw land, farms, condominiums, single family homes, apartments of all sizes, office buildings, warehouses, campgrounds, mobile home parks, hotels, motels, restaurants, factories, dock facilities, health clubs, used car lots, etc. Every conceivable kind of real estate format has been encountered in the various FSLIC receiverships throughout the United States.

Each FSLIC receivership typically has a varied combination of asset formats available for sale to the general public. These include performing loans, financial paper, securities, nonperforming debt, personal property, and real estate owned. Performing loans are marketed and sold as individual loans or as portfolios collateralized with real estate. Nonperforming loans are found in various stages of default, litigation, or restructuring. All assets are being prepared for marketability.

Before Assets Can Be Sold

In order to market any real estate asset, a seller must be able to transfer a clear and marketable title to the property. The most common means of acquiring ownership and extinguishing title blemishes is foreclosure. Foreclosure is specifically provided in the loan documents that the borrower executes at the time of purchase.

Foreclosure actions vary from an extremely brief version in Texas to lengthy processes that include the right of redemption in Colorado.

A popular response for a person or entity facing foreclosure is to file for bankruptcy. The filing of a bankruptcy petition operates as a stay, or judicial suspension, against all creditor actions involving the debtor's property. Property of the debtor includes all legal and equitable interests and is broadly interpreted by the courts. Therefore, any entity filing bankruptcy with legal title or partial interests in property will stop a foreclosure. Actions for collection of debt, which are also liberally defined by the courts, include written and oral demand for payment, posting for foreclosure, acceleration of debt and, of course, any act to foreclose or repossess collateral. Creditor action against the debtor's property or activity to collect a debt of the borrower without Bankruptcy Court approval is punishable as contempt of court with the possibility of severe penalties.

Until the legal complexities of each asset are thoroughly evaluated, asset managers cannot discuss preliminary information about a particular asset with potential purchasers. The risk of lawsuit for meddling in a borrower's affairs and upsetting any sales potential orchestrated by the debtor is too great. The marketing function can begin only when the bankruptcy stay is lifted, the foreclosure process is completed, and the receivership actually possesses clear title. This assumes that preliminary and final business plans have been approved while the above procedures are concluded.

How Are Real Estate Sales Prices Determined?

Once the final business plan is approved by the National Review Committee, the asset manager technically should have the authority to accept any sales offers in conformance with the terms established in the final business plan. If the present value of net cash proceeds is greater than the adjusted NRV per the approved disposition strategy, then the receiver should accept the proposed sales contract. This has not been the case in the real world.

In early 1987 the General Accounting Office (GAO) was conducting an internal audit of California receivership operations and completed real estate sales. The GAO audit team could not comprehend why the receivership ordered new appraisals, yet deeply discounted the appraised values to arrive at the net realizable value. Wasn't this a waste of taxpayer/creditor monies? Why couldn't the appraised value serve as the NRV and the NRV calculation nonsense be eliminated? Without understanding the concept of future discounted cash flows, that GAO audit team influenced FSLIC liquidation procedures. They did not understand that discounting today saved the costs of carrying real estate during the estimated holding period. Before the GAO audit, FSLIC receivers sold properties at NRV plus associated holding costs to the date of closing. After the GAO audit report, FSLIC-OLD mandated that all sales be completed at 90 percent of current appraised value or better. That single policy has had an extremely profound effect on FSLIC receiver real estate sales.

However, it is not entirely equitable to give the GAO audit team report complete responsibility for the FSLIC's sales price policy change. Other market forces influenced this decision, including the FADA/FSLIC controversy and congressional inquiries into dumping assets at fire sale prices. Despite the necessity to sell property and replenish the FSLIC insurance fund, Congress was sensitive to the disruption of local real estate market values. To add further controversy, the FADA boasted it could sell property for even more than appraised value. With all the turmoil, the FSLIC-OLD created a policy mandating receivership assets must be marketed with an asking price of 100 to 110 percent of appraised value. There could be no final sales price under 90 percent of appraised value unless formally approved by Local and National Review Committees.

Special Warranty Deeds/"As Is" Condition

Recent lawsuits have placed greater emphasis upon the seller's warranty of real property condition. REO usually consists of situations where the failed savings institution or its successor, the FSLIC as receiver, has no detailed knowledge of the property's faults. There is no reasonable means of determining problems after foreclosure action since the real estate is frequently vacant or partially occupied. Lack of knowledge has proven to be an inadequate defense in future lawsuits.

The FSLIC has developed several methods to alleviate this potential liability. The most important remedy is to transfer property title via a Special Warranty Deed. A Special Warranty Deed warrants and represents good and marketable title from the date the FSLIC took ownership. No warranties are made by the FSLIC prior to legal acquisition of each asset. For real property, the burden of prior-to-acquisition title warranty rests with the title company providing title insurance.

Another safeguard utilized by FSLIC receivers is to require an "as is" condition clause in each earnest money contract or offer to purchase. Although this requirement is frequently shirked by potential buyers, the inclusion of this verbiage is mandatory for almost all FSLIC receivership real estate sales. The language states that the seller makes no warranties, expressed or implied, as to the condition of the land or improvements constituting the property. The purchaser accordingly agrees to accept the property at closing in an "as is" condition.

FSLIC Loan Portfolio Marketing

The loan portfolio marketing process is a combination of analysis, organization, valuation, and marketing. Each receivership loan portfolio is usually assigned to an outside valuation consultant experienced in the appraisal of mortgage portfolios. The contractor performs an unbiased analysis of all loans in the portfolio. A receivership asset manager then incorporates the loan valuation report into a business plan, which must be approved by Local and National Review Committees before marketing can commence.

While larger portfolios require more time, the average portfolio analysis takes five to seven weeks. Because receivers offer only limited representations and warranties, the evaluation process usually includes 100 percent documentation review of all loan files, not just a random sampling.

To calculate the NRV of the loan portfolio, the portfolio must be stratified into categories based on collateral type and current/delinquent status as of the valuation date. Applying market conditions, an estimate is made of the additional yield a prudent investor would require from the loans in the receiver's portfolio to compensate for the associated risk. The added risk is due to factors including geographical location, poor underwriting, delinquency status, and the lack of FSLIC guarantees.

The value of loans delinquent over 90 days is based primarily on collateral value. There is no well-established market for delinquent loans. Prospective purchasers of these loans typically determine value from the collateral they anticipate receiving at foreclosure, less estimated foreclosure costs. This value will then be discounted to provide the investor with a reasonable return for the amount of time it takes to see the loan through foreclosure and the sale of collateral. In addition, an investor may anticipate litigation upon foreclosure and reserve for that contingency. Consequently, the estimated sales price of loans over 90 days delinquent will typically be considerably less than the current appraised value of the collateral.

The loan portfolio business plan includes the proposed marketing plan and budget. Based upon the plan, information packages are prepared using the approved pooling (grouping of mortgages for sale) methods. The package contains sufficient data for a prospective purchaser to make a bid proposal. Potential investors receive summary information on delinquencies, principal balances, locations, property types, appraisal data, and other relevant loan and collateral facts. Bidding instructions include a confidentiality agreement required upon bid submittal. The initial package is designed to prequalify buyers before sending more comprehensive material and permitting bidders to review files.

A confidentiality agreement is required from any potential purchaser of receivership loans who desires to review loan files. The document requires the purchaser to acknowledge the confidential nature of the file information. Procedures are specified for review activity, originals and copies, debtor contact, conflicts of interest, breaches of agreement, and stipulated damages. The agreement is necessary to safeguard receiverships from the liability of interfering in debtor affairs prior to foreclosure.

The last procedure is the bidding process. In order to reach a broad market response, the receiver frequently will advertise in local newspapers and trade magazines. A single receiver contact person is designated to coordinate inquiries. Each prequalified buyer, as determined above, is provided with individual loan information on the portfolio or pool and access to the files for due diligence activities. Potential buyers are typically given one month to respond with bids. Bids are analyzed and contract awards are generally made to the highest bidder. Profuse negotiation results from the deteriorating nature of the assets.

How the FSLIC Markets REO

The FSLIC as receiver uses a number of marketing techniques to market foreclosed real estate on a regional and national basis. The major thrust of the liquidation effort begins at the receivership level. There are no better informed or qualified experts than the special representative/managing officer and the receiver's asset managers. Because they must manage the assets on a daily "hands on" basis, they frequently have more current and complete information pertaining to a specific property. Receivership staff directly report to FSLIC Regional Offices. Their efforts are monitored by the FSLIC-OLD in Washington, D.C.

Foreclosed real estate sales methods are similar to the successful sales procedures for any property. The first step is the installation of a "for sale" sign. Prospects must know that the property is available. Advertising in local newspapers is utilized sparingly by each receiver to hold down costs. Despite the minimal advertising, hundreds of telephone calls are answered weekly by receivership asset managers responding to data inquiries. After preliminary asset data is given, each caller is directed to send a written request for further information. The written correspondence is then logged to facilitate tracking and forwarded to the appropriate asset manager or agency. Purchasers are advised that offers to purchase must be submitted only on FSLIC receivership pre-approved contract forms. Documents have been developed for improved, unimproved, condominium, and single family properties. The forms include provisions for 60 day contract periods, substantial earnest money deposits, nonassignment of the contract, and a 30 day FHLBB approval contingency.

Each receiver participates in an FSLIC regional and national listing of real estate properties available from the FSLIC Regional Offices in Dallas, Los Angeles, and Washington, D.C. Revised and distributed bimonthly, the listings are disseminated to regional data bases of interested purchasers that include regional, national, and international buyers. In addition to the FSLIC Regional Offices, the FADA also produces a monthly property list for the assets it manages.

Both of these publications are designed to provide only summary information. If after reviewing a prospectus a potential buyer desires additional information, the specific receivership representative is listed with a telephone number. Each of the prospectuses request future investors to complete buyer profile forms. Their purpose is to qualify buyers and add names to the FSLIC buyer mailing directory.

In September 1987 the FSLIC took a new marketing step with the opening of a Central Region Marketing Center. Located in the Dallas, Texas joint office of the FADA and the FSLIC, the facilities are designed to enlighten the public about the $7 billion-plus of FSLIC assets for sale nationwide. The center includes slide and video presentation areas. It was created to represent the FSLIC's intensified commitment to provide investors access to real estate and loan portfolios acquired from failed institutions. The office is open to the public for viewing and discussing available properties with marketing personnel.

Investigations into alternatives to the traditional retail real estate sales procedures have continued. Among the alternative strategies for disposing of foreclosed properties are auctions, bulk sales, lotteries, sales incentives, and joint ventures with equity participations. Although auctions represent an efficient means to get firm contracts on many assets quickly, the associated price discounts have posed problems for the FSLIC. With bulk sales, the seller offers a package of assets to buyers searching for an income-producing return. The subsequent buyer's bid usually includes a 20 to 40 percent discount to cover rehabilitation, packaging risk, and a preferred return for equity investment. Joint venture proposals provide unique approval concerns because of the buyer's required financial strength and long-term commitment.

Real Estate Brokers and Commissions

The most basic method to market real estate is the use of real estate brokers. Unfortunately, the FSLIC and the FADA do not utilize the brokerage community as effectively as possible. Exclusive listing agreements for desirable properties are infrequently and inconsistently given to brokers. It is difficult to discern why brokers are left out in the cold. One reason could be a coordination problem between the FSLIC, the FADA, and their contract asset managers. Another might be the strong desire of the FSLIC, the FADA, and contract asset managers to prove their exclusive marketing skills. FADA and FSLIC contract management firms usually receive a disposition fee when an asset is sold. Those fees provide contractors extra income. Despite these turf struggles, a larger percent of brokers must play a greater role in the FSLIC's marketing effort. The FSLIC must liquidate assets as efficiently as possible. That goal must include brokers.

FSLIC-OLD policy has been to exclusively list those assets which lend themselves to local market exposure and promotion, such as single family dwellings and future development tracts of raw land. All brokerage firms submitting proposals to exclusively list FSLIC assets are carefully screened. Market analyses by two or three local brokerage firms are solicited before a selection is made and presented to the Local Review Committee for approval. The selected firm is then required to submit specific company profile information. This detailed data includes biographical, corporate, financial, and other pertinent reports.

A standard listing term is 90 days. The broker must provide monthly activity reports. After 90 days, performance is reviewed and the listing is either renewed or transferred.

Although the standard brokerage commissions for FSLIC receivership properties vary, the following schedule lists sales commissions that have been approved in the past:

R.E.O. Type	Commission
Raw Land	Negotiable up to 5%
Commercial Property	Negotiable up to 3%
Multi-family	Negotiable up to 3%
Single-family homes	6%

The above fees are typically lower than the acceptable norms in the private sector. The only exception is single-family homes, which sometimes are included in local multiple listing services. The commissions are gross percentages of the final sales price. If there is more than one broker, the multiple parties split these fees. Commissions for commercial office and retail leases and financed transactions are frequently negotiated even lower. The FSLIC believes that when a tenant or buyer renege on a long-term lease or financing transaction, FSLIC receivers should not be left holding the bag while a broker has received all of his fees. Holding the bag means the FSLIC will have paid out the full commission at closing yet a sale or lease deal will fall out after the closing. Thus, the sales or lease commission must be paid once again to solicit a new buyer or tenant. Commissions are usually paid at the closing of the transaction.

Other Kinds of Assets, Personal Property

Whenever a savings and loan association is closed by the FSLIC, the personal property inventory of furniture, fixtures, and equipment becomes available for liquidation. The normal practice is to allow receivership staff the right to use necessary office furniture and equipment in receiver operations. The remaining office assets are offered to the new de novo savings and loan, if applicable, or else they are sold on the open market. The variety of personal property found at closed thrift offices is endless. There have been automobiles including Mercedes, valuable art work including notable paintings and sculpture, jewelry, computers, china, silver, and country club memberships.

As with real property, normal disposition procedure for personal property begins with an appraisal based upon liquidation at market value. The appraiser is a recognized expert in the required field. After the appraisal is reviewed and approved through the business plan process, the property is put up for sale. The sale process will depend upon the existing interest and the relation of submitted offers to appraised value. If the offers equal or exceed appraised value, the highest bidder is the winner. If no acceptable bids are encountered, the asset is advertised and held until a qualified bid is received.

Subsidiary Corporation Businesses for Sale

Upon the appointment by the Federal Home Loan Bank Board of the FSLIC as receiver, the receiver becomes sole shareholder of first tier subsidiary corporations. In turn, the first tier subsidiaries typically own, in whole or in part, second and third tier subsidiary corporations. Although these entities are not technically in receivership, the fact that the financial institution has been closed and creditors must be paid demands that the FSLIC maximize its return. Most often, the highest return is affected by the sale of the subsidiary corporation interests.

Receivership subsidiary assets have included automobile dealerships, trust companies, security brokerage firms, currency exchanges, oil and gas operations, ski resorts, insurance agencies, various charter series, aircraft ownerships, and numerous real estate development concerns. Savings and loan associations have occupied the status of shareholders, general partners, limited partners, guarantors, lenders, or any combination of the foregoing. Each of these relationships allows the receiver to assert certain rights which provide the opportunity for the receiver to recover its investment in the entity.

The receiver is, whether as an investor or lender, similar to subsidiary creditors and is entitled to the liquidation proceeds of the subsidiaries' assets. However, the receiver must be cautious in its efforts to recapture its investment in or loans to subsidiaries. It must avoid situations where other creditors will challenge such activity in the event of bankruptcy. Potential causes of action include preference, fraudulent conveyance, and a variety of lender liability claims. The above terms are bankruptcy law theories that control debtor asset activity before and after the debtor seeks relief under the bankruptcy code. The receiver can also be subject to claims of bad faith as either a partner, shareholder, or lender. These would include breaches of fiduciary duty to other partners, failure to act properly as a lender, or mismanagement of the entity.

Liquidation of subsidiary corporations can be accomplished in several ways. The most advantageous form of disposition in terms of removing receivership liabilities is a stock sale. A stock sale provides the relief that no lingering liabilities exist other than those associated with the sales document. Although the stock sale is the cleanest form of sale, it is the most unlikely form of transaction. Purchasers are often deterred by the potential existence of unknown corporate liabilities that would survive the transfer of stock. An alternative approach is to offer certain assets of the subsidiary for sale.

FSLIC Seller Financing Availability

The issue of the FSLIC as receiver financing the sale of foreclosed real estate has been heatedly debated throughout the Bank Board System for years. The center of the problem is the extensive amount of real estate obtained through the foreclosure of mortgage liens securing loans made by failed financial institutions. Due to the depressed real estate markets of the Southwest, receivers have had a difficult time completing the traditional liquidation method of cash sales. The FSLIC's ability to provide competitive financing has enhanced its efforts to sell property. Many institutional lenders are preoccupied with their own nonperforming real estate and will not extend financing on any terms. The frequent usage of financing to facilitate the sale of FSLIC-controlled real estate has widened the market for the REO sales to include the small entrepreneur who is skilled in turning around difficult properties. By providing seller financing, the FSLIC has significantly increased the number of potential purchasers.

FSLIC financing has been controversial because each receivership is supposed to have only a two to three year liquidation life span. Much like a bankruptcy trustee, the receiver's life is designed to end when the affairs of the estate are substantially wound down. However, if the receiver sells property to buyers for cash and notes secured by the REO properties, what happens to the notes? Does it make any difference if the notes have three, five, or twenty-five year terms? By accepting mortgage notes, the FSLIC entangles the liquidation of a receivership estate. On the other hand, the ability to sell foreclosed property (and thus generate cash proceeds) is hampered by the lack of competitive financing for such sales especially in the depressed Southwest.

Several times during the 1980s, the FSLIC approved the sale of receivership mortgage loans to be incorporated into mortgage-backed securities. In each instance, the FSLIC in its corporate insurance capacity guaranteed timely payment of principal and interest on those loans. The sales involved portfolios of seasoned existing mortgages originated prior to the closing of the failed savings and loan. There has only been preliminary discussion concerning how to market mortgage loan paper resulting from the sale of FSLIC receivership REO.

Feasibility for the disposition of REO paper has also been hampered by the recapitalization of the FSLIC. With the Financing Corporation entering the debt markets for billions of dollars and the Southwest Plan obligating the FSLIC for even more, there has not been a clear directive issued by FSLIC as to how to proceed. Bank Board senior managers have wavered in the past about whether purchase money mortgages should even be accepted. During 1986 and the first half of 1987, only cash sales were considered for receivership assets. As the savings and loan crisis deepened and FSLIC senior management changed, the emphasis shifted to generate purchase money mortgages. The seller financed mortgage notes supposedly could be pooled with other receivership paper throughout the United States. This collateral would then become FSLIC equity in the Southwest Plan. However, the FSLIC was not able to utilize the REO mortgage paper as planned.

Much confusion exists regarding FSLIC policy to use mortgage notes. The FSLIC thought process has been influenced by market realities. Overbuilt real estate markets allow only selected all cash sales because few financial institutions will provide REO financing. Sales volume in these regions would decrease dramatically if FSLIC seller financing was eliminated. Only a delicate balancing act between FSLIC financing and cash sales will achieve the highest return to creditors. The FADA, the FSLIC, or specific receiverships were never created or funded to hold foreclosed assets for long periods of time. The orderly yet steady disposition of REO will help stabilize real estate market equilibrium and provide the creditors a prudent return.

Currently, each receiver financed sale is negotiated by the receivership asset manager who is specifically assigned to the asset. It is the asset manager's role to complete an underwriting package on the buyer which includes a credit report, financial statement, bank reference checks, and a determination of whether or not the potential purchaser was financially involved with the failed thrift. The assembled information is then included with a summary of the asset's approved business plan and routed to both the Local and National Review Committees. The process normally takes 30 to 45 days when no major objections are raised by the committees. After a financed REO sale has been approved, either the asset manager or the receivership's loan servicing department services the loan. Processing and required documentation are coordinated and managed by the asset manager and fee counsel, although in-house FADA counsel has been used by the FADA from time to time.

Regulations establishing formal policies and procedures have not been implemented for the sale of properties with term financing. However, because the National Review Committee must give final approval, consistency in terms and conditions has resulted. Each proposed sale is negotiated and approved on a case-by-case basis. The review committees have attempted in all cases to set broad policy guidelines which are modified to meet regional market demands.

Down payments have varied from a low of 10 percent to a high of 50 percent or more. A lower down payment requirement results in a higher sales price and a larger pool of potential investors. Requiring a significant down payment ensures a purchaser's commitment to a project and discourages highly leveraged speculators from bidding on FSLIC properties.

Terms to maturity have ranged from three to ten years. Maturities of up to five years address the holding periods for most land parcels, but longer maturities are necessary for Southwest land deals. Nonresidential REO properties are by nature illiquid because of the absence of an established secondary market for that mortgage paper.

Monthly payments are typically required yet consideration is given to the fact that foreclosed property frequently has no current operating cash flow. Such loans might require interest at a market rate with 50 percent of the interest paid currently by the borrower and the balance accrued to principal. A typical receivership mortgage consists of level total debt service payments based on a 20 to 30 year amortization schedule, with a balloon payment (remaining principal balance) due at maturity.

Interest rates are determined by blending the FSLIC's cost of funds and existing market rates. Stepped rate structures are rarely accepted by the FSLIC. An example of this would be a contract in which the interest rate begins at 5 to 6 percent and escalates to a 10 percent interest rate over a five year period.

Personal guarantees for REO financed debt are usually not required because buyers simply will not agree to the idea. Consequently, a buyer's financial strength (cash flow, liquidity, and real assets) weigh heavily in the approval process. A successful track record and clean credit report are also necessary.

Chapter 9.

WORKING WITH THE FSLIC
THE KEY TO PROFIT

FSLIC Working Conditions

To understand the current FSLIC environment, this book has spent considerable time and effort explaining the structural organization and procedures of the Federal Savings and Loan Insurance Corporation and its Operations and Liquidations Division. Ominous economic conditions have been compounded by feuding interests between Congress, the thrift industry, the FDIC, and FSLIC department policies. However, the FSLIC System has worked well in defiance of the constant barrage of criticism. As in all large organizations, the foremost objective is to administer the corporation's affairs in a businesslike and sensible manner. That can be extremely difficult at times when countless distractions arise due to political concerns. The FSLIC has not always made perfect decisions and thus has not always pleased all parties. But all Americans must admit that the FSLIC has fulfilled its mission for the past 50 years to ensure safety and soundness in the thrift business. One of the main ingredients for that success is the dedicated staff of the FSLIC.

The human resources element of the FSLIC consists of two divisions. The first includes the 1,200-plus federal government employees based in Washington, D.C., working officially for the FSLIC in its corporate capacity. The second segment is the 900-plus receivership employees. Technically, they are contract personnel hired to liquidate receivership assets of failed thrift institutions throughout the United States. FSLIC contract employees are personnel hired for an indefinite time span. They are not considered Federal government or FSLIC employees. Contract employees also make up part of the FSLIC Regional Office staff. Much controversy has resulted from this two tier system. Critics have charged that the FSLIC is illegally attempting to circumvent the OMB and the OPM Federal government hiring and wage limits by staffing receiverships with contract employees. However, the true facts portray a congressionally mandated receivership liquidation process that cannot perform unless it has sufficient staffing.

Efforts to rectify the unusual status of these contract employees have had mixed results. The most recent attempt has been to centralize receiverships and their associated operations into the FSLIC regional offices located in Los Angeles, Dallas, and Atlanta. Each of the remaining three regional offices will be staffed with thirteen key federal employees to whom the contract employees will report. These Bank Board supervisors will strictly control the day-to-day operations of the contract staffers.

Although the contract employee system exhibits certain disadvantages, it also provides major benefits. Length of employment is determined solely upon the receivership's needs. Employment contracts clearly state that the employee is subject to termination at any time without cause. Personnel are counseled that their sole purpose is to liquidate the receivership estate. By accomplishing that mission, they will eventually be working themselves out of jobs. There are no promised Federal government employee benefits such as grievance procedures or pensions.

Some of the difficult issues FSLIC-OLD receivership employees must deal with are totally foreign to the private sector. A potential purchaser or service contractor can more easily purchase property or provide services by understanding what factors influence each FSLIC decision. By stepping into FSLIC employees' shoes, the businessman will realize that the receiver's hesitancy to act is not slow motion, but rather a conscious effort to work within procedural guidelines. Anyone desiring to work with the FSLIC must develop the same patience and perseverance required in a large government institution.

A Political Animal

The FSLIC, like any other governmental agency, is influenced by politics. Upper level management of the Bank Board is subject to change after each presidential election because the chairman of the FHLBB is appointed by the President. New chairmen usually install fresh executive management. These high level managers in turn promote new policy initiatives, which often conflict with existing procedures. This transition can require lengthy periods of time. In the interim, lower and middle management are often unsure about what procedures should be followed.

Members of the Senate and House of Representatives also affect FSLIC operations, both in Washington and in the field offices. They respond to concerns voiced by their constituencies, either privately or through formal congressional inquiries directed at the FSLIC. When a congressional inquiry is tendered by the Bank Board Congressional Relations Office, senior managers in FSLIC operating divisions must respond immediately. This means prioritizing a response before addressing daily receivership operations. Oftentimes the issue in question is insignificant when compared to the importance of the total FSLIC receivership mission. In many cases, constituents report only portions of the facts to elected officials. After portraying the FSLIC as a large governmental bureaucracy, protests are raised about FSLIC authority. Frequently, these complaints are last minute attempts by borrowers to prevent the foreclosure of their property. Elected officials' office staffs investigate the allegations because of concern about the FSLIC's ability to competently handle the transactions. The FSLIC receivership typically substantiates its case and proceeds with the approved legal action. However, much time and energy is expended by FSLIC personnel answering issues, often needlessly.

Authority Vs. Accomplishment

Governmental organizations rely upon a defined chain of command. While supreme authority governs from the upper levels, the daily decision making is concentrated in the field. Within certain clearly defined parameters, middle and lower managers and their staffs effectively administer operations. Because of the lengthy time delays encountered when soliciting upper level management approval, middle managers try everything humanly possible to operate within their established approval limits.

As with any chain of command, there are penalties for insubordination. The desire to accomplish may be tempered with the reality that a superior may be content with maintaining the status quo. There are no incentives in place to foster entrepreneurial goals. The paradox here is that although the FSLIC is charged by congressional mandate to insure and if necessary liquidate failed savings and loans, few incentives are offered to FSLIC managers to encourage productive results.

Lower Pay Scales

As mentioned previously with the FADA, the FSLIC has been unable to consistently attract experienced personnel because of nominal pay scales. Quality staff are mandatory to effectively deal with the horrendous problems associated with bankrupt thrift associations. The daily FSLIC operational headaches can overwhelm the most professional managers. The stakes are high since billions of dollars of troubled real estate and other assets are at risk.

Lower compensation means less experienced people. That does not necessarily signify that the field staff of the FSLIC is incapable of handling the situation. It does equate to more junior managers who are unsure of their duties and the assets they must control. These managers must grow into their positions. More time is then required to grasp the complexity of the assets.

Inferior pay scales only work to decelerate the liquidation process. With less experienced staff, the potential for errors increases. To lessen the likelihood of mistakes and the resultant criticism, the FSLIC has relied upon the committee process even more than before.

Management by Committee

Due to congressional accusations of judgment errors, the committee approval process is used extensively at the FSLIC. Decision making is handled by groups consisting of five or more senior managers. As committee makeup changes, committee decisions adapt accordingly. Past precedents do not necessarily dictate future actions. The most significant effect of FSLIC committee action has been the potential for inconsistent and sometimes improbable decision making. Because receivership business plans, bankruptcy actions, and foreclosure decisions are never straightforward, issues regarding the negotiations of participation loans, buy-outs of underlying liens, and sales contracts can lead to profuse discussion. Anything can happen!

In all fairness, it should be pointed out that the issues each committee member faces are controversial. Frequently, there is no right answer and obvious logic may not prevail because cross examination may raise additional objections. There is no textbook available that can efficiently define the correct course of action in a severely depressed market for REO. The committee may review and decide 10 to 50 agenda items per meeting. With so many issues, meetings have lasted for several days. Approvals get easier toward the end of the meeting.

With Bureaucracy in Mind

Understanding the bureaucratic process is extremely important to be able to work effectively with the FSLIC. Anyone desiring to conduct business with the FSLIC must be able to appreciate the endless operating constraints imposed by a host of variables. Each FSLIC employee, whether a federal employee or contract manager, must conform to those factors in order to exist in the system. Outsiders desiring to solicit FSLIC business must be able to understand the bureaucratic obstacles and empathize with the FSLIC employees' plight.

A dose of common sense is also appropriate. It is senseless to needlessly harass FSLIC receivership managers. Receivership staff must comply with established policy and procedure. No matter how logical a proposal appears to an outsider looking in, a managing officer and his staff are limited to following procedures. As noted previously, only by working with and through the system can business proposals be approved. With all the conflicting circumstances affecting receivership staff, patience, perseverance, and a desire to cooperate can make the difference is securing a desired approval.

How to Find FSLIC Property

Although finding property may seem like a very simple matter, the fact is that despite all the reorganization within the FADA, the FSLIC, and the Bank Board, no single source exists for asset availability information. One proven method of finding FSLIC receiver properties is to carefully inspect "for sale" signs. A sign displaying a solid background color (usually white), letters in another contrasting color (usually black or blue), and an asset number usually signifies that the FADA or the FSLIC is involved. The signs are generally drab because of cost considerations. To secure property information, buyers can simply call the number listed on the sign.

Another means is to subscribe to the FSLIC Regional Offices' Available Properties Listings. For example, the Central Regional Office of the FSLIC located in Dallas, Texas, is currently actively marketing over $650 million of REO in the Southwest and South-Central sections of the United States. Asset types include office, retail, industrial, motel/hotel, multi-family, and land. The publication is distributed every other month to members of that office's investor data base and is available upon written request. Receivership REO asset information is presented in a stratified format by asset type and location. Once assets of particular interest have been chosen, the listed representative should be contacted. The inquiry will be directed to the appropriate FSLIC manager to forward more comprehensive asset data.

The marketing department of the Central Regional Office requests that each subscriber complete and return an investor profile questionnaire which is included with each prospectus copy. The respective profiles represent both real estate and loan asset interests. This new information serves to identify which market and asset types the buyer has a specific interest. The marketing office then directs information to investors on a selective basis to better meet investment needs.

The FSLIC Central Regional Office address is:

FSLIC, Central Regional Office
5080 Spectrum Drive, Suite 1000 E
Dallas, Texas 75248
214-701-2400

The Western Regional Office of the FSLIC also publishes a similar available properties brochure. Published every other month, the prospectus is presented in a segmented format by product type, such as commercial, multi-family, or land. Once specific properties are identified, the listed entity must be called to receive more comprehensive asset information. In order to continue to receive the available properties brochure every other month, an inquiry card must be returned to:

FSLIC, Western Regional Operations
Marketing Department
523 West Sixth Street, Suite 550
Los Angeles, California 90014
213-623-7055

The Eastern Regional Office of the FSLIC has been scheduled to move to Atlanta, Georgia, to more closely interact with the Atlanta FADA offices. However, that proposed move has been planned for over a year. The only national marketing information listing is available from the Eastern Regional Office. The location is:

FSLIC, Eastern Regional Office
1730 Rhode Island Avenue, N.W., Suite 310
Washington, D.C. 20036
202-955-4530

The FADA also produces a monthly Property List. As a contract asset manager for the FSLIC, the FADA has billions of dollars of foreclosed real estate for sale. The Property List is intended to provide interested parties with preliminary information only. If more detailed data is desired, the inquirer must submit a written request to the FADA. The buyer is also requested to complete a FADA Buyer Profile. Like the FSLIC, these profiles are designed to facilitate the dissemination of more specific asset data to qualified investors.

The FADA Property List contains an abundant use of disclaimers. The brochure explains that while some prices are not listed, they may be established in the future. Potential buyers must also note that although certain properties are under contract, backup offers will be considered. The balance of the disclaimers are designed to prevent claims for incompleteness of the list; guarantees for information accuracy and integrity; and changes, errors, or omissions. Because of numerous FADA locational changes, the best way to obtain information is to call FADA's marketing hot lines:

800-225-3968 (U.S.)
800-621-1219 (Texas)

Although the FADA and other contract asset managers are listed as key contacts for certain assets in the available property listings, it is important to determine exactly which receivership owns a specific asset. That information is crucial for a number of reasons. Purchase offers require ownership information. Sometimes the only way to ascertain the true status of a project and its marketability is through the receivership special representative. A special representative is authorized person who can execute a sales contract or a deed. The best advice is to always contact the listed asset manager and courteously request the necessary property information. Buyers must work with the designated representatives patiently. If that communication becomes unworkable, then the purchaser should not hesitate to contact the special representative as another resort.

A prospective buyer may not be able to determine which receivership owns a property or who is the contract asset manager. The reasons for a delay in FSLIC ownership can vary from an automatic stay in bankruptcy court to fierce litigation. When the FSLIC manager states that the FSLIC owns the property, a more precise investigation must be undertaken. Although the FSLIC in its corporate capacity as an insurance corporation does hold title to real estate, that possibility is rare considering the volume of receivership assets available throughout the United States. A title company or other ownership source, such as a municipal taxing agency, should then be contacted to determine exactly which FSLIC receivership has title. It is important to know exactly who has ownership so that valuable time is not wasted on an asset that may not become available for sale for years.

Recent FSLIC-OLD and FADA Reorganizations

In June of 1988, the FADA formally announced the implementation of an internal organizational study. The review included a reexamination of purpose and an evaluation of existing corporate structure. Special consideration was given to asset management economies and the value added by the FADA. Numerous dialogues between regional managers and FSLIC personnel proved invaluable in the analysis of the number of regions, location of regional offices, asset assignment to regions, functional versus portfolio structure, and the nature and location of central office functions.

The FADA study recommended increased asset management efficiency, operational cost reductions, and improved public information flow. To accomplish those goals, FADA Regional Offices faced major reorganization. The FADA study strongly recommended that FADA Regional Offices exist in the same cities as FSLIC Regional Offices. The FADA San Francisco corporate offices were closed. The FADA Denver Regional Office became a field office. Functional modification of the FADA's remaining offices included the establishment of a Dallas loan participation group and the relocation of the mainframe computer facility and appraisal data base to Dallas, Texas. A new FADA Eastern Regional Office would open in Atlanta, Georgia. FADA corporate accounting was relocated to Washington, D.C. Individual asset accounting and reporting became decentralized into the regional offices. FADA address and telephone data, reflecting these changes, is listed in the Appendix.

The FSLIC-OLD was also reorganized with the FADA's changes in mind. The FSLIC Northwest Regional Office (Seattle, Washington),

Central Regional Office (Chicago, Illinois), and the Eastern Regional Office (Washington, D.C.) were downsized to FSLIC Area Offices. Personnel and operations in the existing FSLIC Los Angeles and Dallas Regional Offices increased substantially. A new FSLIC Eastern Regional Office will be opened in Atlanta, Georgia, to interact with FADA's new Eastern Office in that same city. FSLIC field offices include Houston, Texas; Metairie, Louisiana; Little Rock, Arkansas; Salt Lake City, Utah; and Boynton Beach, Florida. Revised FSLIC Regional Office address and telephone information is included in the Appendix.

As part of a concerted effort to improve the resolution of failed thrift institutions, the Office of General Counsel also plans to open offices in Atlanta, Dallas, and Washington. Each office will consist of two real estate attorneys, a paralegal, and a secretary. The Office of General Counsel plays an important role in daily receivership operations. Whenever an extraordinary legal aspect arises, an OGC attorney must be apprised. By evaluating the consequences of any receiver activity to federal receivership law, the OGC attorney levies significant legal control.

How to Purchase FSLIC-Controlled Real Estate

The Preliminaries of a Purchase

After a particular real estate asset has been selected for further review, the buyer must obtain as much information as possible from the asset manager. The potential purchaser should try to remember the virtue of patience and understand that the property under review is most likely a foreclosure. There may not be much available information. Furthermore, desperate borrowers oftentimes plunder an asset, so that stoves, refrigerators, carpeting, air conditioning/ heating systems, and maintenance equipment are removed and sold for scrap or salvage prior to a foreclosure sale. The receiver or its asset managers may not know about these losses. For that reason an "as is" special warranty deed is used to transfer title. Another concern to the receiver is the distribution of operating and income statements, security deposit ledgers, and other data supplied by former debtors, which often provide a misleading financial picture. The receiver certainly does not want to deceive any buyer. Each receivership is apprehensive about the quality of available data. Nonetheless, buyers should remember to ask for all available property data and inspect the property if possible before submitting an offer to purchase.

As the initial information gathering process proceeds, any involved broker should inquire about the commission structure available. The larger receiverships sometimes require a formal information request and a written agreement signed by the buyer authorizing the broker's representation. Brokers should keep in mind that an asset's approved business plan has already fixed the available commission to be paid. Usually the commission is lower than the going market rate and not negotiable. Any changes require committee approval and are subject to lengthy delays.

Extra effort should also be given to determine exactly what the asking price represents. FSLIC receiverships have sometimes been instructed to ask or list a property at 110 percent or higher of appraised value. Others ask for 100 percent of the appraised value. Assets throughout the FSLIC receivership system can be sold for 90 percent of appraised value. It pays to ask for the 90 percent value, but do not be surprised if the asset manager remains mum and simply repeats his asking price.

Written Offers to Purchase
As the buying process continues, new questions must be posed by the buyer or his representative and answered by the asset manager. Each receivership throughout the United States has an assigned legal counsel. Therefore, every receiver has different idiosyncrasies regarding sales contracts. Certain states have significantly different forms of sales contracts which can include earnest money contracts or offers to purchase. Because of these variations, it is extremely critical to ask the asset manager for a copy of the receivership's approved purchase contract forms. Each buyer's unapproved contract forms (including Multiple Listing Service contract forms) will most likely require study and approval by the receiver's legal counsel. Unusual cases demand review by the receiver's Washington Office of General Counsel representative. That process could take weeks and still be subjected to the review committee process. By

utilizing each receiver's pre-approved purchase contract forms, considerable time can be saved and the buyer will not have to guess the necessary FSLIC sales contingencies. The approved forms simply require filling in the blanks.

Considerable debate has arisen regarding the use of letters of intent to purchase FSLIC assets. A letter of intent is a written document in letter format that carefully, yet simply, defines the buyer's basic terms and conditions for a proposed purchase of an asset. Some buyers refuse to transact business unless their letters of intent have been formally accepted. The problem with letters of intent is they seldom contain all the terms and conditions mandated by the receiver's legal counsel. After the basic letter has been accepted, another round of negotiations must commence to finalize the multi-faceted sales contract. Some purchasers demand acceptance of a letter of intent before engaging their attorneys to begin sale negotiations. However, the most efficient way to purchase FSLIC-controlled property is to forego a letter of intent. Purchasers should proceed with the completion of the receiver's approved offer to purchase form. This practice will expedite the approval of the offer at the review committee level.

The proposed offer to purchase should be based upon the purchaser's preliminary due diligence, although FSLIC sales have included 30 to 90 day inspection contingency periods. During these inspection intervals, the buyer is permitted to perform a variety of engineering and feasibility studies at his expense. The required initial down payment to prove a buyer is earnest is held in escrow until the buyer waives the inspection contingency and any other contingencies or conditions of the contract. Typical contingencies entail physical inspection and review of operating data (if available), soil tests, title policy, termite inspection, survey, plans and specifications, etc. The earnest money dollar amount will depend upon the asset's size.

Preliminary discussions with the FSLIC should also involve the question of financing. FSLIC receivers offer financing for some but not all assets. A purchaser must ask what terms are available. (Refer to Chapter 8, "How the FSLIC Really Sells Assets," for a complete discussion of financing.) Within the offer to purchase include, within reason, the desired financing terms and conditions.

The entire process of negotiating and completing an offer to purchase must include the assigned asset manager. That asset manager must be satisfied that the offer is fair and equitable since he or she will present the offer to the receiver's special representative. Technically, if the offer is for cash and is 90 percent of appraised value or higher, the special representative should be able to approve the transaction and sign the contract. However, recently the policy in several FSLIC Regional Offices has been to send all offers, regardless of type, to the review committee process. The asset manager might also advise the buyer about sale activity, title defects, and other closing problems.

Underwriting Requirements for Financing

To receive FSLIC financing approval, the borrower should submit a satisfactory financial statement if acting as an individual borrower, statement of the corporate officers for a corporate borrower, or statements of each general partner if the borrower is a partnership. The financial statement should be dated within 90 days before the date of the proposed closing. If the borrower is a corporation, its balance sheets and profit and loss statements for the previous two years, certified by an officer, are required. If the borrower is a partnership, its balance sheets and profit and loss statements for the previous two years, certified by a general partner are required.

If the borrower will manage the mortgaged premises, the addresses of other properties managed by the borrower, the number of units, and condition of the properties should be included. If a management firm will manage the mortgaged property, a description of the firm including the number of years in business should also be submitted. Other data should include the type and variety of assets managed, along with the total estimated number of units.

The receivership asset manager orders a written credit report on the borrower issued by an independent credit reporting agency. The report verifies the borrower's present employment and income. The asset manager confirms all financial statement debts and all legal information, including lawsuits, judgments, foreclosures, garnishments, bankruptcies, divorce action, etc. discovered by a search of public records. If the credit bureau does not verify current employment and income, the borrower is asked to provide written verification. Bank references are requested of all parties.

The receivership's underwriting analysis also stresses the following issues:

1. Knowledgeable management which will work to keep the property competitive, maintain the property at adequate standards, and relate the cost of overall operating expenses to collectible rent/lease levels. The borrower must recognize the difference between essential repairs and optional maintenance that may improve net income to the property on a continuing basis.

2. Thorough analysis of the borrower's credit worthiness. There should not only be strong evidence of ability to repay the mortgage but also a history of making mortgage payments according to the terms of other loans.

3. Careful analysis of the borrower's financial statement to determine the borrower's equity position, particularly as it relates to real estate investments, real estate mortgage debt, and attendant mortgage demands on equity.

4. If the borrower's holdings are heavily encumbered so that the debt service requirements consume a high percentage of the rental income, care must be exercised to determine that the borrower will be able to meet the mortgaged premises' loan obligations (expenses, debt service, and equity return).

Review Committee Approval Procedure

The sales contract, buyer's financial data, and earnest money check should be submitted as a package to the asset manager. The asset manager then consults with the special representative. A decision is made to approve or reject the purchase offer or send it to committee. A preliminary financing committee consisting of Federal government Regional Office staff will review and approve FSLIC seller financing proposals. If it is approved by the financing committee, the asset manager must then request to be placed on the next Local Review Committee agenda. Local Review Committees meet once a week; however, there are stringent submittal deadlines which must be met. A Local Review Committee can approve the sale of assets below $10 million without further action. Sales in excess of $10 million or those involving special financing must also be approved by a National Review Committee, which meets once a month, or an Executive Review Committee, which meets via teleconference in emergencies.

The property's asset manager or the special representative are the only persons eligible to appear at the committee meetings to obtain approval for the offer to purchase. Receiver staff must feel comfortable that the deal will be good for the receivership, since they will be subjected to intense questioning. For financing requests, committee members carefully review financial statements to determine ability to pay. Current occupancy reports are analyzed with the approved business plan budget. This review determines whether the financial resources of the borrower are sufficient to make debt service payments and necessary capital improvements. Anything suggesting further questions has the potential to derail the approval process until the next meeting. The loan evaluation process is comparable to a senior loan committee review at a large bank.

Completion of the Sale
After the appropriate review committee approvals have been obtained, the purchaser can proceed to complete the release of all contingencies. The asset manager returns an executed sales contract to the purchaser. The receiver expedites the delivery of a final survey and title policy to the buyer. The process to rectify title objections raised by the purchaser begins. The sales procedure continues with the receiver providing additional available financial information, such as the most current rent rolls and operating statements. Finally, after all the conditions of sale are waived, legal counsel proceeds with drafting of the closing documents.

The closing of a sales transaction is normally held at the offices of the receivership's legal counsel. Closing documents are signed by the special representative preceding the actual closing. The asset manager and legal counsel are customarily present at the closing.

FSLIC Vendor Selection for Goods and Services

The selection process for goods and services in the FSLIC receiver-ship system consists of a complex interaction between the Bank Board, District Banks, FSLIC Regional Offices, and the FADA. With so many entities to deal with, where does a contractor start? What agency, department, regional office, receivership, asset management contractor, or managing officer must be found to actually sign a contract? This section will investigate the receivership contracting system to provide helpful and profitable hints to crack this complex program.

Due to the various levels of FSLIC involvement, contracting can be best described as fragmented. To determine how contracts are obtained, it is necessary to understand various FSLIC procedures. The closing of a failed savings institution begins at the national level in Washington, D.C. With the guidance of the regional District Bank supervisory personnel, a decision based upon hundreds of previously described factors is implemented to effect a merger or liquidation. However, prior to that final edict, endless preliminary strategy planning has been ongoing. Frequently the institution in question has been operating under a Management Consignment Program (MCP), where participant thrifts are managed by other healthier savings and loans. Under the MCP, the managing institution, under the direction of the District Bank and the FHLBB, exercises considerable power in determining operational policy and contractor selection. Types of services required include legal counsel, financial consultants, asset management, and property management. It is difficult to be more specific because the Management Consignment Program is actually a holding pattern for a future course of action to be determined. A primary objective is to maintain the status quo. The contractor selection process is divided between the FHLBB, the District Bank, the MCP manager, and the failing thrift's surviving management.

As the time draws nearer to liquidation, the Office of General Counsel starts soliciting bids for legal counsel. Asset management contract bids are requested from the FADA and other private sector contractors from the OLD. On the actual day of the failed thrift's demise, the legal counsel and asset management functions have already been decided by the FHLBB and the OLD. Thereafter, the receivership's asset managers and special representative, under the guidance of an FSLIC Regional Office and the FSLIC-OLD, are responsible for the day-to-day operation of the liquidating receivership. The contracting for goods and services is then divided among the FSLIC Regional Office, the FADA, the receiver's asset managers, and the special representative. Additional sources of influence can include the FSLIC-OLD and the District Bank.

The Washington Connection

Many contractors have asked how to find the Washington Connection. The truth is that there is no such animal. To be really successful in developing Washington contacts takes years of hard work and an abundance of good luck. No matter how much effort is expended, each new presidential election ushers in fresh new Bank Board senior managers. The new faces combine with other influences to complicate contractor/vendor selection issues even further. The only proven means of scaling the Washington mountain is to be successful in a specialized field of endeavor. Professionals become known because of their reputations. The asset management companies and legal firms presently employed by the FSLIC are regionally known for their outstanding work. They have survived the rigors of FSLIC assignments. Yet to get started, most were chosen by being at the right place at the right time with a great reputation.

In 1988 the FSLIC reorganization plan established a receivership Contracting Administration Division to be based in Washington, D.C. The position is designed to oversee the procurement of contractor services throughout the FSLIC receivership system. Although specific duties are unclear, the Division reportedly will only review contracts. Initial screening and final selection will still be made at the receivership level. Because of increasing Federal government concerns for equal opportunity, much emphasis is being placed on diversifying the contractor base.

District Bank Vendor Registry Programs

Several of the Federal Home Loan Banks have instituted vendor registration programs to provide member savings and loan institutions a computerized evaluation of pre-screened contractors available in their service areas. The programs are designed to identify providers of the following services:

Real estate loan workout
Real estate disposition
Project management
Property management
Loan refinancing
Real estate loan underwriting
REO portfolio management
Other troubled loan workout
Other loan underwriting
Loan underwriting procedures
Security portfolio analysis
Asset/liability management
Business plan development
Asset classification
Loan portfolio management
Appraisal
Appraisal review
Market/feasibility analysis
Financial/economic analysis
Other asset disposition
Cash management
Auditor/financial consulting/accounting procedures
Information system consulting
Human resources management
Strategic planning
Architectural/structural engineering consulting
Loan versus investment classification
Mortgage servicing
Mortgage banking evaluation/development
Litigation management
Other service types

The process has been engineered as a referral system. Although the District Banks do not approve or endorse contractors, they do furnish a summary of qualified bidders upon request from a member savings institution. The District Banks will respond to a member's query with a three page computer profile on each qualified contractor. The requesting savings and loan then calls the vendors and solicits bids. If a potential contractor is not in the District Bank's data base, obviously the vendor cannot be included for bidding.

To make application to the vendor registry program, a contractor should call the closest District Bank and request a questionnaire form. The questionnaire is fairly detailed. It requires disclosure of individual or corporate ownership, experience, financial data, and specific expertise. If an individual is applying as a consultant, a resume, financial statement, and two years of income tax returns are also requested. A listing of the District Banks in the Appendix includes pertinent telephone numbers and addresses.

FADA and FSLIC Regional Office Vendor Registration

In addition to the Federal Home Loan Bank contractor advisory programs, both the FADA and the FSLIC have separate vendor selection programs. Each entity performs extensive background checks of the principals of the applying vendor company. Recently, the FADA and the FSLIC have attempted to simplify the application process by utilizing the same contractor registration request form. The current Contractor Registration Request is a simplified version of the original Questionnaire for the Federal Asset Disposition Association which frequently alienated applicants. The initial questionnaire was similar to a loan application, demanding highly confidential financial and business details. Larger organizations had to spend profuse amounts of time to complete all the fill-in blanks. The new format,while still comprehensive, is much more appropriate. The submittal of a contractor application is acknowledged by return mail.

The Contractor Registration Request attempts to more specifically categorize a contractor's skills and locational preferences. Five general service categories include (1) Property Management, Maintenance, and Leasing; (2) Brokerage and Marketing; (3) Planning and Construction; (4) Consulting Services; and (5) Appraisals. The subdivision of the service categories provides the potential contractor the ability to select areas of expertise from the following listing:

Property Management, Maintenance, and Leasing

Property Management
Condominiums
    0 - 10 Units
    11 - 80 Units
    81+ Units
Hotel/Motel
    0 - 80 Rooms
    81 - 200 Rooms
    201+ Rooms
Industrial
    Bulk
    Special Purpose
Land
Low-Income Housing
    Subsidized
    Non-Subsidized
Marina
Medical
Mini Warehouse
Mobile Home Parks
Multi-Family
    2 - 80 Units
    81 - 500 Units
    501+ Units
Nursing Homes
Office
    Garden
    (Under 100,000 s.f.)
    Mid-Rise
    (100,000 - 300,000 s.f.)
    High-Rise
    (Over 300,000 s.f.)
Resort/Golf Course/Athletic Club
Retail
    Strip
    Mall
Single-Family
Time-Share
Restaurant
Church
School

    Airplane
    Boat
    Farm and Ranch

Leasing
    Agricultural
    Apartment Locators
    Equipment Leasing
    Multi-Family Leasing
    Office Leasing
    Retail Leasing

Security Service
    Drive-by Security
    Electronic Security
    Guard Dogs
    On-Site Security
    Security Guards

Property Maintenance
    Acreage Mowing
    Apartment Turns (Make Ready)
    Building/Site Maintenance
    Janitorial Services
    Landscape Maintenance
    Locksmith
    Pool Service/Repairs
    Signage
    Window Cleaning

Brokerage and Marketing

Real Estate Brokers
    Condominiums
        0 - 10 Units
        11 - 80 Units
        81+ Units
    Hotel/Motel
        0 - 80 Rooms
        81 - 200 Rooms
        201+ Rooms
    Industrial
        Bulk
        Special Purpose
    Land

Low-Income Housing
  Subsidized
  Non-Subsidized
Marina
Medical
Mini Warehouse
Mobile Home Parks
Multi-Family
  2 - 80 Units
  81 - 500 Units
  501+ Units
Nursing Homes
Office
  Garden
  (Under 100,000 s.f.)
  Mid-Rise
  (100,000 - 300,000 s.f.)
  High-Rise
  (Over 300,000 s.f.)
Resort/Golf Course/Athletic Club
Retail
  Strip
  Mall
Single-Family
Time-Share
Farm and Ranch

Marketing/Sales
Aerial Photography
Auctions
Business Brokers
Direct Marketing—Sales
Property Signage
Syndication
Auto, Boat, Airplane—Sales
Public Relations
Advertising

Planning and Construction

Tenant Finish Out
Construction Consulting
Construction Draw Certification
Construction Inspection

    Construction Management
    Construction Review & Analysis
    Cost Estimate & Analysis
    Project Management & Supervision

Environmental Consulting
    Asbestos Management
    Environmental Engineering
    Environmental Impact Studies
    Environmental Site Assessment
    Hazardous Waste Management
    Industrial Hygiene Survey

Surveying
    As-built Survey
    Topographical Survey
    Boundary Survey
    Construction Staking
    Architectural/Engineering Consulting
    Architecture
    As-built Drawings
    Civil Engineering
    Construction Documents
    Design & Engineering
    Electrical Engineering
    Energy Management
    Interior Design/Decorator
    Land Planning
    Landscape Architecture
    Mechanical Engineering
    Physical Plant Evaluation
    Roofing
    Soils Engineering/Geotechnical
    Space Planning
    Structural Engineering
    Traffic Engineering

Construction
    Asbestos Removal
    Carpentry/Millwork
    Clean-up/Board-up
    Demolition
    Electrical
    Excavating/Paving
    Fencing

Flooring/Carpet
General Contracting
Hazardous Waste Removal
HVAC/Mechanical
Landscaping/Irrigation
Masonry
Miscellaneous Repairs
Painting
Plastering
Plumbing
Roofing
Structural Repairs
Building Supplies
Utility
Weatherizing
Windows/Glazing

Real Estate Consulting
Asset/Project Management
Development Planning
Feasibility Studies
Financial/Economic Analysis
Highest & Best Use Studies
Market Analysis
Owners Associations
Platting Process
Site Observations
Time-Share Analysis
Zoning

Consulting Services

Accounting, Auditing, Financial Services
Blind Shoppers
Financial Consultants
Financial Fact Finding
Financial Projections
Audits
Cash Management

Financial Investigation
Asset Searches
Credit Reports
Lien Searches

      Private Investigators
      Skip Tracing

Property Tax Consulting
      Property Tax Reductions
      Delinquent Tax Searches
      Abstractor's Certificates
      Agricultural Use Exemptions

Real Estate Consulting
      Asset/Project Management
      Development Planing
      Feasibility/Studies
      Financial/Economic Analysis
      Highest & Best Use Studies
      Market Analysis
      Owners Associations
      Platting Process
      Site Observations
      Time-Share Analysis
      Zoning

Other Consulting
      Farm, Ranch, Livestock
      Oil & Gas
      Inventory & Floor Plans
      Strategic Planning
      Human Resources Management
      Legal Services

Loan Administration
      Asset Classification
      Collections
      Loan Analysis/Underwriting
      Loan Funding Audits
      Loan Policy & Procedure
      Loan Servicing
      Loan Workout
      Repossessions
      Commercial Secured
      Commercial Unsecured
      Asset/Liability Management
      Credit Card

Title Work
      Title Policies
      Title Updates

Asset Management
  Business Planning
  Asset Analysis
  Loan Portfolio Analysis
  Securities Portfolio Analysis
  Market Analysis

Insurance
  Appraisal
  Condominiums
      0 - 10 Units
      11 - 80 Units
      81+ Units
  Hotel/Motel
      0 - 80 Rooms
      81 - 200 Rooms
      201+ Rooms
  Industrial
      Bulk
      Special Purpose
      Manufacturing
  Land
  Low-Income Housing
      Subsidized
      Non-Subsidized
  Marina
  Medical
  Mini Warehouse
  Mobile Home Parks
  Multi-Family
      5 - 80 Units
      81 - 500 Units
      501+ Units
  Nursing Homes
  Office
      Under 100,000 s.f.
      100,000 - 300,000 s.f.
      Over 300,000 s.f.
  Resort/Golf Course/Athletic Club
  Retail
      Strip
      Neighborhood Mall
      Regional Mall

Single-Family (1 - 4 Units)
Time-Share
Farm and Ranch
Personal Property
    Furniture, Fixtures, Equipment
    Art, Jewelry, Antiques
Market/Feasibility Studies
Expert Witness

Each application requests minority-owned business information. The form includes an acknowledgement whereby the applicant agrees to hold harmless in any capacity the FSLIC, the FADA, the FHLBB, and its member institutions against any and all claims arising from use or dissemination of the information submitted. A registration request may be refused if it contains incomplete or inaccurate information. Anyone who supplies false or inaccurate information that has the effect of influencing in any way the action of a Federal Home Loan Bank, the FHLBB, the FSLIC, the FADA, or any member institution is subject to the penalties set out in Title 18 of the United States Code.

The prospective contractor's completion of the registration does not mean approval or endorsement by the FSLIC or the FADA. Despite the disclaimers, it has been routine for special representatives to be advised by FSLIC Regional Office personnel not to sign a contract because the vendor did not file a registration. Any contractor of services and goods is highly recommended to complete the Contractor Registration Request. As stated before, a sound dose of patience and understanding is often necessary to work with the bureaucracy. The failure to complete a contractor registration could veto a potential contract. The extra paperwork required to avoid such a debacle will be well worth the effort, especially as the FSLIC activates the liquidation process and opportunities expand.

Thought must also be focused on the fact that as the inevitable closing of a greater number of bankrupt savings institutions increases, the approval process will lengthen. Eventually, potential new contractors will overburden the screening process. The resultant time delays can be avoided by making application as soon as possible. Applications can be obtained from the appropriate

District Banks. The Appendix of this book provides a complete listing of District Bank data.

Who Has Controlled Contractor Decisions in the Past?

The special representative or managing officer of the FSLIC as receiver for the failed thrift institution has been charged by the Bank Board with responsibility to cost effectively liquidate the receivership estate. The special representative employs on a salary or fee basis such persons that are necessary to carry out its functions. Costs for such services are paid from the liquidation proceeds of the receivership estate. The managing officer, under the close supervision of the FSLIC Regional Office Director and the FSLIC-OLD also has been accountable for contractor approvals.

There are several qualifiers to the above statement. These involve Chairman's Order Number 613, FADA contracts, and the new federal employees as FSLIC Regional Offices. Chairman's Order Number 613 is an FSLIC delegation of authority memorandum authored on December 3, 1985, and subsequently amended. Its purpose is to specify spending authority for Managing Officers, Regional Office Directors, and OLD Chiefs. Although Order 613 may require additional higher level approvals, the special representative requests and implements the approval authority. An exception is the situation where the FHLBB, through the Office of General Counsel and the Operations and Liquidations Division, has executed attorney and asset management contracts before the thrift is closed.

Another qualifier to the managing officer's authority is the existence of a FADA asset contract. The FADA asset management contract provides for the FADA to be the receiver's attorney-in-fact and grants almost unlimited power to FADA contract managers. The description of FADA authority begins with the right to exercise or perform any act, power, or obligation that the receiver has or may acquire the legal right, power, or capacity to exercise in connection with the assets. Further rights include the ability to lease, purchase, or acquire real or personal property as said attorney-in-fact may deem proper. The FADA can lease, manage, or improve the assigned receivership assets as it deems appropriate. About the only rights the FADA contract does not possess are the powers of a receiver, which entail repudiation of executory contracts, indemni-fication, and the adjudication of creditor claims. Even so, the receivership managing officers have had an extremely difficult time trying to control FADA contracting decisions.

The third qualifier revolves around the installation of Federal government employees at FSLIC Regional Offices. Although their authority is unclear, the FHLBB intent is to delegate more contracting and purchasing decision-making authority to these employees. How this will be implemented remains a question.

Because the contractor selection and approval process is in transi-tion, it is paramount that potential contractors establish rapport with the FADA, FSLIC regional personnel, and the special representatives. All three entities must work together to successfully perform the receivership mission.

Common Sense Advice for Contractors

The selection of a vendor by FSLIC receiverships can take a long and treacherous path. Confusing procurement programs are as difficult for the managing officer and his staff as they are for future contractors. Contractors should empathize and try to comprehend the receiver's plight. Underpaid FSLIC managers are only trying to do their jobs. Oftentimes receivership personnel could use some moral support. But more important, the FSLIC asset managers can only employ contractor ideas and services if the FSLIC staff know the potential vendors.

One of the most common complaints receivership asset managers voice is the failure of contractors to continue to solicit receiver business after the first refusal. Contractors must realize that as the liquidation process of a failed thrift commences, contracting activity initially experiences a lull because of organizational hiring, litiga-tion, and bankruptcy delays. Managing officers do not have the time to interview contractors. But as the receivership gets on its feet, more opportunities for contractors become available. This does not mean that there is a shortage of applicants. However, qualified contractors are always difficult to hire. Future contractors must realize that soliciting new business requires successful advertising strategy. The most effective new business solicitation campaigns employ a consistent program to accomplish name recognition. Regular twice monthly correspondence or meetings that professionally describe personal or corporate accomplishments are recognized much more than a single one time, give-me-the-order interview. Economic or market data for local, regional, and national real estate is also appreciated. FSLIC asset managers can implement this data in business plans and other receivership reports dealing with problem real estate. A concerted effort to pass along real estate market data can pay big dividends by keeping a contractor's name highly visible and helping the FSLIC perform its mission.

Property Management Pitfalls to Avoid

Caution must be used when performing property management for the FSLIC or the FADA. Problems can arise frequently because of the FSLIC's strict interpretation of receivership powers to repudiate executory contracts. In plain English, that means that any existing signed contract for services, including property management, that was executed prior to the date of a failed thrift's closing can be cancelled by the FSLIC as receiver. This situation will occur with thrifts involved in the Southwest Plan, Management Consignment Program, or FSLIC/FDIC supervision.

The Southwest Plan, correctly described to the public as a merger strategy, actually converted insolvent to-be-merged savings and loans into receivership to accomplish the merger. By creating a receivership, numerous outstanding and expensive contract obligations were cleansed from the thrift's books. The FSLIC had to spend less to guarantee potential acquirers a fixed return when the FSLIC could effect lower monthly operating expenses.

The tragedy of this policy is that innocent vendors in depressed markets got hurt. The FSLIC or the FADA hired property management companies to manage a property for a failing thrift. The FADA signed the management contract and directly dealt with the property managers' activities. Within months the insolvent thrift was taken into receivership or merged into the Southwest Plan by the FSLIC. After this action, the management company was told by the FADA to submit all unpaid bills prior to the closing date to the

FSLIC as receiver for payment. The bills in question included utilities, payroll, subcontractor bills, supplies, or anything necessary in the daily operation of an apartment complex, office building, hotel/motel, or specialty project. Requests were submitted to the FSLIC as receiver or to the new Southwest Plan acquirer. The FADA or the FSLIC refused to pay anything but the utility bills. Due to a failed thrift's closing neither entity was legally obligated to pay bills incurred prior to closure. The management company, however, was held responsible because its staff was on-site. To make matters worse, contractors had difficulty filing liens against the property or the FSLIC to force payment of the debt.

The lesson to be learned is to ensure that a property management firm's contract with the FADA or the FSLIC includes some teeth. The management contract should allow the management company to legally claim a lien on the property's cash flow to pay itself and other creditors that the property manager employed. But more important, the contractor must use a little common sense. The contract should give management fees top priority before paying any other charges out of the real estate's monthly cash flow. A contract manager should compensate his company first before all the operating funds are gone.

If Everything Else Fails, Call Your Congressional Representatives

A vendor or contractor that follows the suggested procedure of courtship to solicit FADA/FSLIC/FDIC business or purchase property may not always find success. Even after all the correct actions have been taken, bureaucracy frequently bogs down. When everything else fails, a contractor should not hesitate to contact his elected congressional representatives' offices. If all legitimate methods have fizzled and available patience has been exhausted, elected officials in Washington, D.C., may be just the catalyst to undermine a contract bottleneck. Congressional staffs are experts in ferreting out the reasons for bureaucratic gridlock. If the complaint is relatively legitimate, a congressional inquiry will be issued to the FHLBB's Office of Congressional Relations. That Office's strategic mission is to dissolve problems and answer formal written inquiries from congressional staffs. The Bank Board Congressional Relations personnel typically request a formal written answer from a receiver within several days after receipt of the elected representative's correspondence. Although timeliness of the inquiries may vary, the constituent can be assured that the managing officer, FSLIC Regional Director, and FADA asset managers, if applicable, will be alerted to the investigation. Responses will include an explanation of the problem and a prognosis of the ultimate solution.

The use of elected officials should not be the normal, everyday mode of business operation. If everyone yelled fire continuously, the system would deteriorate and become useless. As a last gasp attempt to retain sanity, an elected representative and his staff can ensure results.

Chapter 10.

THE FEDERAL DEPOSIT INSURANCE CORPORATION (FDIC)

Early Banking Legislation

The early American settlers possessed a sincere desire for freedom. They risked everything to explore the New World and escape from persecution and tyranny. The colonists wanted independence and minimal government control. Many settlers came from countries where a central government bank monopolized financial markets. The immigrant's fervent desire for free enterprise caused the opposite effect. Anyone who wanted to open a bank could do so. Initial requirements were simple. As a result, banks opened and closed their doors with ease. There was no Federal government bank chartering system.

The colonists' use of gold and silver pieces (hard currency or species) was a major problem because there was not enough of these metals. Notes were issued that supposedly could be redeemed for hard currency. Unfortunately, confusion developed from counterfeiting and the refusal by some banks to pay on demand. In 1791, Alexander Hamilton convinced Congress to open the First Bank of the United States to solve the currency crisis. Despite the Bank's efficiency, colonists worried about the central government bank becoming too powerful. In 1811, Congress vetoed the First Bank's charter renewal.

A second Bank of the United States opened under a 20 year charter in 1816. Congress failed to renew its charter in 1836. The lack of a central bank created chaos. Fraud, massive counterfeiting, and poor service diminished public faith and trust to its lowest point ever. Conditions grew worse as Congress failed to act. Finally, President Abraham Lincoln, strapped with huge Civil War costs and a need to raise funds, promoted an overhaul of the banking system. The National Currency Act was passed by Congress in 1863 and amended as the National Banking Act in 1864. These Acts provided for (1) new financial institutions called national association banks, (2) reserve requirements for deposits and notes, (3) a uniform type of currency called a national bank note, and (4) a new Treasury Department Office called the Comptroller of the Currency.

Congress intended state-chartered banks to join this national system. Rigorous qualifying requirements and congressionally mandated lending standards promoted soundness. The Office of the Comptroller of the Currency (OCC) was created to enforce these guidelines. The national bank notes promoted public confidence, raised government revenues, and regulated each bank's debt leverage.

The Federal Reserve Act of 1913

As the U.S. continued to grow in the early 1900s, banks like savings and loans, experienced growing pains although different in nature. The lack of a check collection system caused confusion and needless delays. The nation's money supply was hampered by a legal limit ratio of national bank notes to government bonds in circulation. To overcome these problems, the Federal Reserve Act was enacted in 1913. The Act divided the U.S. into 12 districts, each with its own Federal Reserve District Bank. Member banks could send out-of-town checks directly to the appropriate Federal Reserve District Bank. The Federal Reserve received authority to issue notes without government obligation backing. It could make loans to member banks under certain conditions, thus providing the economy with a source of funds.

The Federal Reserve Act presented banks a choice since state-chartered banks were allowed to remain outside the Federal Reserve

System if they so desired. State-chartered banks could join and resign at a later date. National banks, required to become Federal Reserve members, could withdraw at any time to become state-chartered banks.

A Comparison of the Federal Reserve System and the Federal Home Loan Bank System

The Federal Home Loan Bank System (FHLBS) was established in 1932 and modeled after the Federal Reserve System (FRS) which was created in 1913. Both systems have 12 District Banks which are wholly owned by their member institutions. Each District Bank has a separate board of directors supervised by an independent government agency board in Washington. District Bank presidents in both systems are elected by their own boards of directors and confirmed in Washington.

In each system, some directors are elected by member institutions while others are appointed by the Washington boards as general public representatives. All directors in both systems promote the public interest. Federal Home Loan Banks have fourteen member boards at a minimum while Federal Reserve Banks have standard nine member boards. The Federal Reserve Board of Governors has seven members, while the Federal Home Loan Bank Board has only three board members.

The FRS was created as the U.S. central bank. It is responsible for directing monetary policy as the nation's lender of last resort. As world markets have grown with technological advancements, the Federal Reserve has become the world's central bank with the dollar's emergence as the world's reserve currency. The FRS operates the U.S. check processing and electronic payments networks. It also regulates commercial member banks and bank holding companies.

The FHLBS has more restricted responsibilities. The Bank System was directed to advocate the specific goal of home ownership within the thrift industry. There is no similar job description in the FRS. The FHLBS Banks play a greater role in member thrift operations. The District Banks are a significant source of funding for thrift members. In contrast, the Federal Reserve discount window is seldom used by commercial banks since it was not designed to be a frequent source of bank funds. Another unique difference is the direct correlation between FHLBS performance and member institution dividends. FHLBS dividends contribute substantially to member thrift earnings. FRS dividends, on the other hand, account for only a small share of member bank earnings. The bulk of FRS earnings are returned to the U.S. Treasury.

The FHLBS is supervised much more stringently than FRS members. The FHLBS presidents, as the principal supervisory agents for the Bank Board, are more involved in district activities than FRS presidents. However, because the FRS dictates U.S. monetary policy through the Federal Open Market Committee, FRS presidents influence national economics beyond district boundaries. The FHLBS has no parallel opportunity to influence national or international monetary policy.

The Banking Act of 1933—The Birth of the FDIC

In 1930, 1300 U.S. commercial banks failed and by 1933 over 8,000 bank closures caused deposit losses in excess of $7 billion. Unemployment was rampant. Depositors could not withdraw their funds because the banks simply did not have the money. In 1933 Congress reacted with a bill that restored public confidence in banks while significantly altering commercial bank operations.

The Banking Act of 1933 imposed new bank charter application restrictions, prohibited interest on demand deposits, forbade underwriting of corporate stock issues, and set interest rate limits on forms of time deposits. Yet its most important provision was the establishment of the Federal Deposit Insurance Corporation (FDIC). The FDIC was designed to (1) initially insure bank deposits of $2,500, (2) set guidelines for member bank operations, (3) examine banks to ensure compliance, (4) take action to prevent bank failures, and (5) pay depositors and liquidate failed banks.

FDIC History

The FDIC was chartered by Congress in the Banking Act of 1933 as an independent agency of the Federal government. The FDIC opened for business on January 1, 1934, at the height of the Great Depression, following a banking crisis that saw thousands of banks close.

The FDIC's first and most urgent task was to help restore public confidence in banks. The FDIC's insurance function was quickly buttressed by the development of a bank supervisory program that to this day reduces risk to the FDIC's insurance fund by fostering safe and sound banking practices. Protection of bank depositors continues to provide an important stabilizing influence on the economy.

A comparison of the number of bank failures before and since establishment of federal deposit insurance provides a measure of its achievement.

From 1900-1919, an average of 82 banks failed each year. The number rose to 588 per year during the generally prosperous roaring twenties. In the Depression years of 1930-1933, the number of failures rocketed to an average of 2,277 per year. The climax came in 1933 when some 4,000 banks closed their doors.

After the introduction of deposit insurance on January 1, 1934, the number of bank failures declined. From 1934 through 1942, failures averaged 43 per year. Most of these casualties were unsound banks that reopened after the banking holiday of 1933. Subsequently, the failure rate declined markedly. From 1943 through 1985, failures totaled 482 for the 43 year period, or an average of 11 failures each year. The failure rate in recent years has risen sharply due to economic difficulties from agriculture, energy development, and overbuilt real estate.

Constructive banking laws and the efforts of other federal and state supervisory agencies have played an important part in maintaining stability. A healthy national economy created general prosperity that has prevailed in the decades since the Great Depression. The FDIC has contributed to the restoration and maintenance of the public's banking confidence through improved banking practices.

FDIC Organization Chart

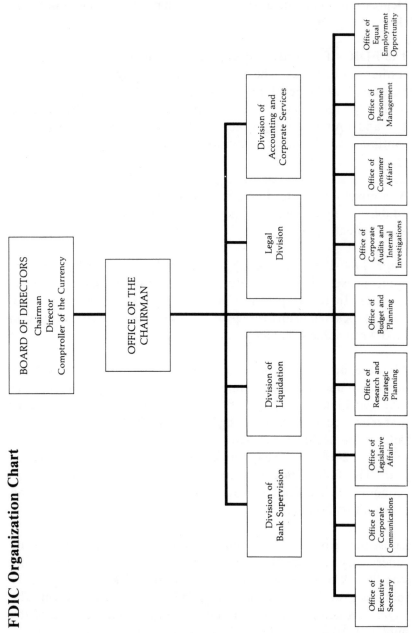

BOARD OF DIRECTORS
Chairman
Director
Comptroller of the Currency

OFFICE OF THE CHAIRMAN

Division of Bank Supervision

Division of Liquidation

Legal Division

Division of Accounting and Corporate Services

Office of Executive Secretary

Office of Corporate Communications

Office of Legislative Affairs

Office of Research and Strategic Planning

Office of Budget and Planning

Office of Corporate Audits and Internal Investigations

Office of Consumer Affairs

Office of Personnel Management

Office of Equal Employment Opportunity

What Is the FDIC Today?

The Banking Act of 1933 created the FDIC as an independent agency which insures deposits at commercial and savings banks. Membership is mandatory for commercial banks belonging to the Federal Reserve System (FRS). All national (federally chartered) association banks belong to the FRS. State-chartered banks which are not members of the FRS have the option of being insured by the FDIC. Membership for savings banks is also optional. Eligible accounts are insured by the agency for up to $100,000. As of July 1988 the FDIC insured 4,477 national banks, 8,934 state-chartered banks, and 470 savings banks.

The FDIC is self-supporting. Member institutions are assessed an annual insurance premium of 1/12 of one percent on the institution's average deposit liability less certain exclusions and deductions. Assessments are collected when insured institutions are audited by the FDIC. The other major source of revenue for the FDIC is the interest income earned on its holdings of U.S. Treasury obligations. In January 1989 the Corporation's insurance fund had approximately $15 billion available to assist or close financially troubled member institutions.

FDIC Organization and Structure

Congress created the FDIC as an independent agency of the Federal government. Although the FDIC receives no appropriated funds, the FDIC is subject to congressional supervision. It annually reports to Congress on its operations. Its chairman appears before congressional committees from time to time at their request to testify on FDIC operations. The FDIC is also subject to audit by the U.S. General Accounting Office. The FDIC's employment practices are conducted within the framework of civil service regulations. The law vests management of the FDIC in a three member board of directors. Two directors are citizens appointed by the President with the Senate's consent for six year terms. One of these appointed directors is elected by vote of the board to be chairman. The Comptroller of the Currency, who serves ex officio as the board's third member, is appointed by the President with the Senate's consent for a five year term. Only two board members may have the same political party affiliation.

The FDIC'S responsibilities are carried out by ten divisions and offices, including the Division of Bank Supervision and the Division of Liquidation.

FDIC Divisions and Offices

Legal Division

The Legal Division furnishes the legal services necessary to enable the FDIC to discharge its duties. The Division drafts and interprets regulations that are required by law. It monitors the performance of outside attorneys hired to represent the FDIC in court actions connected with the liquidation of closed banks. There are thousands of such actions in litigation at any one time. The Division serves as the FDIC's litigation arm, handling proceedings for cease-and-desist actions and other formal enforcement processes.

Division of Accounting and Corporate Services

The Division of Accounting and Corporate Services is responsible for all FDIC finances. Administrative support services include budget preparation, accounting, computer support, facilities management, library services, and printing.

Office of Research and Strategic Planning

The Office of Research and Strategic Planning provides analyses to the board of directors and other FDIC offices. This research includes emerging issues, financial developments, and policy issues related to the FDIC's legislative, regulatory, and administrative activities.

Office of Personnel Management

The FDIC's Office of Personnel Management (OPM) is responsible for the hiring, training, and advancement of FDIC employees. OPM administers employee benefit programs, and sponsors the Employee Advisory Council.

Office of Equal Employment Opportunity

The Office of Equal Employment Opportunity (OEEO) develops affirmative action programs for the advancement of women and minorities in the FDIC's work force.

Office of Corporate Audits

The Office of Corporate Audits (OCA) has complete internal audit responsibility for the FDIC's operational activities. OCA audits assist the board of directors and management in applying resources cost effectively.

Office of the Executive Secretary

The Office of the Executive Secretary (OES) performs corporate secretarial functions. The OES ensures FDIC compliance with the Freedom of Information Act, the Sunshine Act, and the Privacy Act of 1974. As the FDIC's ethics counselor, it administers the Ethics in Government Act of 1978.

Office of Congressional Relations and Corporate Communications

The Office of Congressional Relations and Corporate Communications has a dual role. The Office of Congressional Relations advises the Board of Directors on legislative issues. It prepares testimony and responds to congressional inquiries regarding pending legislation and FDIC operations. The Office of Corporate Communications is the FDIC's contact for banks, news media, and depositors. It generates the FDIC's Annual Report, news releases, and other information.

Internal Committees

Three internal committees advise the board of directors on policy matters. The Board of Review examines all FDIC bank applications. The Liquidation Committee reviews all receivership and purchase/ assumption cases. The Budget and Management Committee decides major policy issues concerning FDIC administrative costs and management practices.

The FDIC's Division of Bank Supervision

Supervision of the nation's more than 13,800 FDIC-insured banks is divided among the FDIC Division of Bank Supervision, the OCC, the Federal Reserve, state banking departments, the Securities and Exchange Commission (SEC), and the Justice Department. Both Federal and state governments can charter commercial and savings banks. Commercial banks with national charters are regulated and supervised by the OCC and insured by the FDIC. Commercial banks with state charters that are members of the Federal Reserve System (state "member" banks) are regulated and supervised by the state regulator and the Federal Reserve, and insured by the FDIC. State-chartered commercial banks that are not members of the Federal Reserve (state "nonmember" banks) and state-chartered savings banks are regulated and supervised by the state regulator and the FDIC if they are FDIC-insured. In addition, the FDIC insures a small number of savings banks regulated by the FHLBB that originated as state-chartered institutions but subsequently converted to a federal charter. The number and asset share of the different types of FDIC-insured banks are shown below.

DISTRIBUTION OF FDIC-INSURED BANKS
June 20, 1988
($MM)

Type	Number	Percent of banks	Assets	Percent of Total Bank Assets
State Nonmember Banks	7,860	56.6	$ 712,959	21.7
Savings Banks (Federal Charter	15	0.1	25,375	0.8
Savings Banks (State Charter	455	3.3	203,554	6.2
State Member Banks	1,074	7.7	541,047	16.5
National Banks	4,477	32.3	1,801,280	54.8
Total	13,881	100.0	$3,284,215	100.0

Each of the above supervisory agencies has its own mission. The FDIC, as insurer, is the only agency directly responsible for maintaining the soundness of the insurance fund, protecting insured depositors, and handling bank failures. The FDIC has authority to examine all insured banks regardless of charter. However, the FDIC traditionally has relied on the OCC and the Federal Reserve for safety and soundness information on national and state member banks. It has restricted examination activity in these banks to specific problem institutions. Equally important, the FDIC has limited rule-making or enforcement authority over national and state member banks, thus severely limiting its ability to protect its insurance interests.

Interagency cooperation is a major FDIC concern. The FDIC with limited regulatory authority over national and state member banks must share the examination responsibility with each state for insured nonmember banks. The FDIC has no authority of its own to charter or close a bank. It must depend solely on its chartering authority to declare a bank insolvent and close it. The FDIC relies upon OCC and Federal Reserve decisions when granting insurance for national and state member banks. It shares responsibility with the states for nonmember banks. The FDIC has veto power over the chartering of insured banks by granting or withholding deposit insurance.

FDIC's Division of Liquidation (DOL)

When an FDIC-insured bank fails, its deposits and some or all of its assets usually are purchased by a healthy institution. The FDIC is empowered to pay off depositors. Insured deposits can be are transferred to healthy institutions. Unpurchased or collected failed bank assets are liquidated by eventual third party sales. These sales reimburse the FDIC and other creditors for any costs relative to net collections associated with the failure. When sufficient funds are recovered from asset sales, other creditors of the failed bank are repaid. These functions are carried out by the FDIC's Division of Liquidation (DOL).

The liquidation of a failed bank's estate can take months or years depending on many factors. The most important variable is the quality of the assets. The First National Bank and Trust Company of Enid, Oklahoma, which failed in November 1986, was liquidated in two months. (All loans were sold in bulk at auction.) The estates of Franklin National Bank, which failed in October 1974, and the First National Bank and Trust Company of Oklahoma City, Oklahoma, which failed in July 1986, will not be settled for some time. Based on asset size, Franklin National and First National Bank and Trust Company of Oklahoma City were two of the largest failures in U.S. banking history.

Faced with mounting bank failures, in 1982 the DOL instituted a five point operating plan to (1) decentralize operations by delegating responsibility to six regional field offices, (2) consolidate liquidation sites, (3) establish formal employee training, (4) develop policies and procedures manuals, and (5) organize strong asset management and marketing programs.

DOL disposition philosophy includes emphasizing settlements and other alternatives to litigation (the FDIC as receiver is heir to a failed bank's pending litigation); ensuring maximum profits from operating assets until they are sold; upgrading automated systems to improve cash management; and carefully monitoring assets under FDIC control.

As part of the liquidation effort of failed bank estates, the DOL uses a team of asset marketing specialists who aggressively seek purchasers for the failed bank's "products" which include loans, real property, and equipment. The DOL's asset marketing staff uses numerous sales techniques. Bundling is the consolidation of specific types of loans for sale. Incentives are popular. If a purchaser is interested in buying a specific portfolio or type of assets, the FDIC will offer a discounted book value provided the purchase includes a "less desirable" group of assets that the FDIC is anxious to divest.

Human Resources

The demand for FDIC supervisory visits combined with increasing liquidation assignments requires a highly trained and motivated examination staff. All bank and thrift regulatory agencies have had problems recruiting and retaining qualified staff. Today, however, the situation is even more critical because of the staggering number of insolvent financial institutions. Over the past decade the agencies have endured hiring freezes, increasing workloads, and high turn-over rates. Much of the problem in maintaining staff stems from salary differentials between the agencies and the private sector.

Recruitment and turnover problems highlight only one side of the staffing issue. Another aspect involves the heightened staff demands in recent years. The enactment of comprehensive civil rights and consumer protection statutes influenced all banking agencies.

Charged with enforcing complex legislative aspects, FDIC management promoted specialty career paths. The FDIC required generalist examiners to take intensive training in the new areas. Specialties such as trust and electronic data processing have placed increased demands on staff resources that traditionally had been earmarked for safety and soundness work. Adding to the foregoing are new pressures on examiners to deal with securities, real estate, insurance, and other activities in which banks may soon be able to engage. To compound matters, the number of problem banks and bank failures has increased dramatically.

The FDIC's safety and soundness supervisory effort was hindered by many examiners being assigned for extended periods to assist in closing and liquidating failed banks. To give a perspective, in 1978 the FDIC had 1,760 field examiners charged with 342 problem banks and 7 bank failures. By 1984 the number of field examiners had declined to 1,389. Although the number of field examiners has subsequently increased to 2,029 as of September 30, 1988, 1,072 are relatively inexperienced trainee or assistant examiners. This inexperienced staff must cope with over 1,400 problem banks. Over 200 banks failed or required assistance in 1988. The Bush administration plan to resolve the thrift crisis would add 350 more insolvent thrift institutions to their workload. To better utilize available resources, the banking agencies have expanded their use of automation and personal computers. Nevertheless, demands on the supervisory staff continue to overwhelm resources.

FDIC and FSLIC Liquidation Staffing
The FDIC has a sizable staff of its own employees working in Washington and in Regional Offices throughout the U.S. In contrast, staff needed for FSLIC liquidation activity are employed on a temporary basis to assist permanent staff. The FSLIC has a staff level of about one eighth the size of the FDIC. The FHLBB performs the overhead functions and the District Banks handle the field work. The FSLIC contracts out more of its receivership operations than the FDIC.

COMPARATIVE STATISTICS OF
THE FDIC AND THE FSLIC
($MM)

	FDIC	FSLIC
Corporate Full Time Staff Equivalents	3,266	383
Total Corporate Personnel Compensation (FY 1987)	$105.7	$13.5
Corporate Administrative/Operating Expenses	$200.8	$25.3
Full Time Staff Involved in Liquidating Assets (as of 2-29-88)	4,072	850
Total Expense for Liquidation Operations (CY 1987)	$401	$228
Book Value of Assets Managed/Liquidated	$12,274	$5,688

When Banks Fail

Whenever a bank becomes insolvent, the FDIC strives to maintain public confidence through banking system stability. The FDIC carefully evaluates the consequences of each closure action on neighboring banks. Bank failure resolutions frequently influence market discipline towards other banks' risk-taking. Another major consideration is cost. By law, the FDIC is required to implement the least costly resolution alternative. The agency must also act fairly and consistently. Uninsured depositors and creditors must be treated equally in large or small bank failures. Community disruption is minimized by swift and professional FDIC action. A major FDIC goal is to minimize the Federal government's role in owning, managing, and financing financial institution assets. All of these objectives are difficult to orchestrate. The trade-offs between stability, cost effectiveness, consistency, and market discipline reduce the FDIC's flexibility. Selection of the most prudent resolution is a complicated process.

Methods of Resolving Bank Failures

There are five basic options available to the FDIC in handling the affairs of a failed or failing bank. These include: (1) deposit payoffs,

(2) purchase and assumption transactions, (3) insured deposit transfers, (4) open bank assistance, and (5) bridge banks.

In a deposit payoff, the bank is closed by the chartering authority. The FDIC is appointed receiver and pays all depositors the full amount of their insured claims. It begins to liquidate the assets of the failed bank. Uninsured depositors and other creditors of the bank generally do not receive immediate reimbursement on all claims. The FDIC distributes receiver's certificates which entitle the holders to a proportionate share of the proceeds from the failed bank's assets. The FDIC also is entitled to a share of these collections since it represents the insured depositors. In the absence of a depositor preference law, depositors, the FDIC, and all other groups of general creditors receive the same proportionate return on their claims.

A second method used by the FDIC to handle bank failures is referred to as a purchase and assumption (P&A) transaction. A buyer purchases all or some of the failed bank's assets and assumes its deposits and certain liabilities. The FDIC invites a number of possible acquirers to a bidders' meeting. A transaction is consummated with the highest acceptable bidder. An important difference between a P&A transaction and a payoff is that in a P&A all depositors, uninsured and insured, receive full payment on claims since their claims are assumed by the acquiring institution. In the absence of a depositor preference statute, general creditors also normally receive full payment on their claims.

A third type of failure resolution transaction is called an insured deposit transfer. Only the insured deposits and secured liabilities are transferred to another institution. Uninsured and unsecured liabilities remain with the receivership. Sufficient cash is paid by the FDIC to the acquiring institution to equal the liabilities minus any purchase premium. Generally, the acquiring institution uses cash to purchase some of the assets. An insured deposit transfer is a deposit payoff variation because uninsured and unsecured creditors are not protected from a loss. However, the transaction has some P&A characteristics. Another institution assumes certain liabilities and, in recent years, usually acquires some of the failed banks's assets. Often high-cost, volatile funds cause bidders to demand an insured deposit transfer. Unlike a P&A, they have the ability to renegotiate debt instrument terms.

The fourth type of transaction is called open bank assistance. Open bank assistance has some of the same effects as a purchase and assumption transaction. The major difference is that with open bank assistance a transaction occurs before the failing bank is technically declared insolvent and closed. Generally, the FDIC provides enough assistance to cover the difference between the estimated market value of the assets and liabilities (the bank's negative net worth). New capital is injected by private investors. As in a P&A , all depositors and general creditors are protected against loss. However, as a matter of policy, management, subordinated debt holders, bank stockholders, and holding company creditors and shareholders are not protected against loss.

A fifth type of transaction is a bridge bank. This solution is temporary. It merely provides a "bridge" until a more permanent solution can be arranged. When a bank fails, it may be advantageous for the FDIC to keep it operating for a brief period. Prospective purchasers should have sufficient time to assess the institution's condition to formulate a reasonable offer. If kept operational, a bank can retain much of its value. Moreover, there is likely to be less disruption to the local community until the situation is resolved through a more permanent solution.

Priority of Claims in a Bank Failure

In order to understand the connection between particular methods for handling bank failures and the FDIC's policy objectives, it is important to distinguish between different groups of creditors and other affected parties, and how these groups are treated when a bank fails. These relevant parties comprise the following eight groups:

1. Insured depositors and secured creditors
2. Uninsured and unsecured depositors
3. Unsecured, nondeposit creditors (excluding subordinated debt holders)
4. Contingent claimants
5. The FDIC
6. Subordinated debt holders and stockholders

7. Bank management
8. Bank holding company creditors and shareholders

The FDIC's paramount responsibility is to safeguard insured depositors. However, as a result of its protection of depositors, FDIC actions also must shield other creditors against loss. Regardless of the FDIC's failure resolution method, some uninsured creditors will receive at least a partial claim reimbursement. The degree to which each group of creditors may or may not be protected against loss when a bank fails has important implications regarding the FDIC's policy objectives.

Of the eight different groups of creditors and other affected parties, four groups almost always suffer losses when a bank fails; three groups occasionally suffer losses; and only one group, insured depositors and fully secured creditors, never suffers a loss when a bank fails. The groups that almost always suffer losses include the FDIC, subordinated debt holders and bank stockholders, bank management, and bank holding company creditors and shareholders.

FDIC Failed Bank Resolution Policy

The FDIC policy is to keep as many failed or failing bank assets as possible in the private sector by attempting to arrange purchase and assumption or open bank assistance transactions whenever feasible. In open bank assistance transactions usually all of a bank's assets are transferred to the acquirer. Similarly, the preferred variation of the closed bank P&A transaction is a "whole-bank" transaction in which all of the bank's assets are passed on to the acquirer. If the FDIC is unable to arrange either of these types of transactions at an acceptable cost test price, it attempts to conduct a more traditional closed bank P&A. Some of the failed bank's assets are passed on to the acquirer, while others remain in liquidation. The next option is an insured deposit transfer, selling as many assets as possible. As a last resort, the FDIC executes a deposit payoff and liquidates all bank assets.

In the past, a purchase and assumption transaction required only a small portion of the failed bank's assets to be transferred to the acquiring institution. These include the best assets: government securities that are marked-to-market, cash, fed funds sold, and the installment loan portfolio. The remaining difference between assets acquired and liabilities assumed is covered by a cash transfer from the FDIC to the acquiring institution. The FDIC must collect as much as possible on the balance of the assets it retains in order to reimburse itself for some portion of its cash outlay.

Today the FDIC attempts to pass a larger portion of a failed bank's assets to an acquiring institution. Substantially all of the failed bank's assets are now sold at a book value discount to the acquiring institution. These "whole bank" transactions are more technically referred to as "total asset purchase and assumption" transactions. The first such transaction was completed in April 1987. Altogether, 19 whole bank transactions were completed in 1987, 65 in 1988 through November.

In the typical whole bank transaction, a one time cash outlay is made by the FDIC to account for the difference between the market value of the assets and liabilities assumed by the acquirer less any purchase premium. After such a cash outlay the FDIC has no further financial obligation to the acquirer. There are no income maintenance agreements or guaranteed rates of return on these assets.

The present FDIC policy has received both praise and criticism. On the plus side, whole bank transactions reduce the need for the FDIC to advance cash to the acquirer and minimize the FDIC's involvement in the liquidation of the failed bank's assets. Such transactions are cost effective and limit the FDIC's private sector involvement. Compared to the more traditional P&A, these resolutions further reduce any disruption to local economic activity. A greater portion of the failed bank's customers continue to have access to banking services and their loans are not placed in a liquidation.

On the minus side, some have argued that the emphasis on P&As and open bank assistance transactions reduces market discipline, preserves overcapacity in the banking industry, and sometimes leads to situations where the FDIC obtains an ownership position in an ongoing institution. The argument against FDIC ownership of banks is that it creates conflict of interest situations and unfair competitive advantages. Inequities remain because the present FDIC failure resolution policies provide for a more consistent treatment of creditors in large versus small banks.

FDIC Asset Disposition

One emerging aspect of current FDIC policy is the emphasis on keeping failed bank assets in ongoing institutions rather than in a liquidation. Certain liquidation costs can be avoided by maintaining assets in a healthy institution. Once out of the bank, assets can lose value quickly. Semi-completed projects that face temporary disruptions in the construction process may lose value. Failed bank assets become tainted due to the bank's association. Liquidation expenses are substantial if the FDIC or another liquidation organization must take control of assets. Unfortunately, all bank failures cannot avoid the liquidation of assets option.

Due to the diverse nature of commercial banking, the FDIC manages and liquidates a wide variety of asset types. Real estate represents over $1 billion of FDIC's total assets. The other real estate (ORE) portfolio comprises a diverse array of residential and commercial properties. In general, FDIC assets reflect the differences between bank and thrift loan portfolios. Failed bank assets are typically smaller and non-real estate collateralized. They include delinquent loans for cars, boats, campers, and unsecured personal and business purposes. Frequently business equipment, office furniture, store fixtures, and inventory are seized from delinquent borrowers and sold by FDIC liquidation personnel. Stocks, bonds, jewelry, art work, and various personal effects are also included.

Real estate assets depend upon the size of the FDIC-insured institution. Larger banks commonly hold a significant amount of real estate assets.

In the disposition process, the FDIC strives to sell acquired properties at market value within six months of acquisition. FDIC liquidators uphold this goal to be consistent with their fiduciary responsibilities. To determine ORE values for marketing purposes, the FDIC relies heavily on appraisals. Every asset of $250,000 or more requires two separate appraisals. Should the two appraisals differ by more than 30 percent, a third appraisal is required. Ideally each asset value is calculated on the basis of a cash sale within six months of asset acquisition with substantial marketing exposure. However, holding costs, market conditions, and asset status are analyzed to compute a discounted estimate of cash flows associated with the property over its holding period. Frequently the six month disposition goal cannot be met. Appraisals are updated on an annual basis.

Shortly before a loan is scheduled to become ORE, the assigned FDIC staff prepare a case memorandum for the appropriate approval level of delegated authority. The memorandum includes the appraisal report and operating budgets. The required FDIC level of approval authority is based upon asset value.

The FDIC liquidation marketing efforts are concentrated in the FDIC's Consolidated Offices, which manage the assets of failed institutions in a specific geographic area. The FDIC presently operates 16 Consolidated Offices nationwide. Six Regional Offices provide oversight and limited marketing support for the Consolidated Offices. The National FDIC Office in Washington, D.C., acts principally in a policy oversight capacity for the Regional and Consolidated offices.

FDIC assets with lesser values can have marketing strategies approved directly by Consolidated Office personnel. Higher valued assets require Regional or National Office approvals.

FDIC Sales Methods

The FDIC utilizes an assortment of marketing methods to sell assets. Listing agreements with local brokers allow the broker's buyer contacts, specific market knowledge, and closing expertise to provide the most expeditious and cost effective disposition. FDIC staff are another sales tool when the assets are within close proximity to the FDIC office. Auctions are used for personal property in bulk, such as office equipment. Inexpensive residential properties, low demand commercial facilities, and raw land tracts also benefit from the auction format.

Another sales method advocated by the FDIC is the sealed bid. Usually the FDIC employs a brokerage firm to conduct a formal sealed bid process. This program involves widespread local advertising. Sealed written offers to purchase must be tendered to the assigned broker by a specific date with earnest money. This sales method, like auctions, generates sales activity. Usually the assets have been available for sale for a period of time. By seeking sealed bids, the FDIC through a broker is actually starting purchase negotiations. The submitted sealed bid amounts are rarely acceptable to the FDIC. Many bidders continue to negotiate with the selected broker to make a deal.

FDIC Sales Guidelines

The FDIC routinely sells a wide variety of real estate that it has obtained in the course of its normal business operations. These properties are offered to the general public without regard to age, sex, religion, or national origin of the purchasers.

All properties sold by the FDIC are conveyed on an "as is, where is" basis. The FDIC neither expresses nor implies any warranties concerning the physical condition of properties, the legal or functional suitability of the properties for their apparent use, or the condition of title. While FDIC information is obtained from sources deemed to be reliable, the FDIC does not guarantee the accuracy of the information. Prospective purchasers are encouraged to thoroughly examine any property offering before transmitting to the FDIC an offer to purchase.

The FDIC does not warrant nor convey title to personal property that might be located on the property or within the dwelling. Personal property includes such items as storage buildings, appliances, window treatments, furniture, automobiles, etc.

The FDIC conveys title to properties being sold by special warranty deed and will pay the cost of owner's title policies if desired by the purchaser. The only other closing charges paid by the FDIC are costs associated with preparation of the deed document, tax statements, pro-rated ad valorem taxes to the date of settlement, and brokerage fees if a provision for brokerage fees is authorized. All other costs of sale are paid by the purchaser at time of settlement. Costs charged to the purchaser typically include attorney fees, filing fees, recording fees, survey costs, escrow fees, documentation fees and taxes, loan origination fees, discount points, appraisal and inspection fees, etc.

The FDIC has become sensitive to the lack of ORE financing, especially in the Southwest. With very few exceptions, no seller financing has been offered by the FDIC. Recently the Addison, Texas Consolidated Office has begun considering financing properties for offers above $200,000. Purchase money mortgages are considered only when no equivalent all cash offer is pending. The financing is not guaranteed until accepted by the FDIC. The FDIC plans to meet market interest rates but with a two to five year balloon payment.

The minimum acceptable earnest money deposit to accompany an offer to purchase is $500 or 5 percent of the offered price, whichever is greater. Any offer to purchase for less than $2,000 should not include any FDIC-paid seller expenses (taxes, association dues, assessments, etc.) except title policy. The FDIC reserves the right to refuse any and all offers associated with the contemplated sale of properties offered by the FDIC. Prospective buyers are requested to transmit their offers using FDIC's approved contract forms. However, legally enforceable written offers in other formats are considered on the individual merits of terms and sales conditions.

How to Find FDIC Properties

The FDIC has developed a uniform approach to the marketing of real estate. Each Consolidated Office publishes a regular (sometimes monthly) listing of available real estate for sale by the FDIC. To subscribe to the list, an inquiry must be made to the appropriate Consolidated Office's ORE Department. After the telephone call, an Asset Marketing Survey—Loans and Real Estate Form will be forwarded to the potential purchaser. The legal size form requests name and address information. The buyer then has the option of making selections for the types of loans and real estate desired. Additional categories specify loan quality, the size of the desired loan portfolio, project income status, occupancy status, and energy related real estate. Geographical areas of interest can also be checked including specific states. A listing of Regional and Consolidated Office data (addresses and telephone numbers) is included in the Appendix.

The primary use of the survey's information is to match qualified prospective investors with specific loan portfolios or real estate for sale. Furnishing the information is voluntary; failure to furnish all or part of the information may result in the prospective investor not receiving notice of a portfolio's availability. Information may be disclosed to other federal or state agencies that also have loans or real estate for sale; to appropriate federal, state, or local agencies for law enforcement purposes; to persons involved in the conduct of judicial or administrative proceedings; and to a congressional office in response to an inquiry made at the individual's request.

Chapter 11.

WHERE DO WE GO FROM HERE?

The FSLIC and the S&L Industry's Current Health

As the FSLIC tried to deal with the increasing thrift institution failures from 1982 to 1986, the reserves of the insurance fund were depleted and the fund became insolvent. During 1987, the FSLIC incurred a net operating loss of $8.6 billion, resulting in a $14 billion deficit—more than double its 1986 deficit. The FSLIC's operating loss was primarily attributable to the $7 billion increase in the FSLIC's liability for failed but still operating savings and loan institutions, and the $3.5 billion in losses for financially assisted and closed institutions. During 1988, the FSLIC's operating losses grew to $17.2 billion for the 217 resolutions of insolvent thrifts completed through December 31, 1988.

In 1986 the FSLIC began in earnest to request substantial recapitalization authority from Congress. On August 10, 1987, after months of debate, the Competitive Equality Banking Act of 1987 was enacted despite overwhelming criticism of the bill's insufficient $10.8 billion resources. The Act provided for recapitalization through the sale of bonds over a three year period.

In its first year, the FSLIC received the maximum amount allowable from the sale of $3.75 billion in bonds, which were issued at interest rates between 9.4 and 10.7 percent. While these additional funds have helped, the FSLIC's cash resources have remained low. At the end of 1987, the FSLIC had cash and Treasury investments of only $2.9 billion. On December 31, 1988, the FSLIC had made financial commitments exceeding its future ten year income stream by $25 billion. Nonetheless, the FSLIC recognizes that the longer insolvent institutions are allowed to continue to operate and incur additional losses, the higher its costs will be. The FSLIC has attempted to quickly deal with many of these insolvent institutions. Since the FSLIC's cash resources are limited, it has been forced to rely upon the use of large promissory notes and other financial commitments in its efforts to support the industry's most troubled thrifts.

The FSLIC's Use of Notes

As of December 31, 1988, the FSLIC's total outstanding note obligations plus interest to thrift institutions totalled approximately $42 billion. This represented a sharp increase in the FSLIC's use of notes in 1988 and a decided shift in the purpose for which the notes were issued. In the past, the FSLIC issued notes payable primarily for two reasons: to assist open institutions in meeting minimum regulatory capital requirements under the Net Worth Certificate and Income Capital Certificate programs, and to compensate the acquirer of a defaulted institution for negative net worth at the time of acquisition.

The balance of FSLIC notes payable issued in exchange for capital certificates rose from approximately $100 million at December 31, 1981, to a high of $2.2 billion at the end of 1985. Since then, the balance steadily declined, totaling only $1.1 billion as of August 31, 1988. In contrast, FSLIC's use of notes in merger-type resolution actions increased dramatically. Between December 31, 1983, and December 31, 1988, its outstanding balance of notes payable to acquirers of failed institutions increased from less than $100 million to almost $38.6 billion.

The FSLIC's Insolvent Thrift Resolution Strategy

The FSLIC has been insolvent for the past two years and continues to conduct its operations at a loss. Its ability to deal with insolvent savings and loan institutions has been severely constrained. The FSLIC is authorized at its sole discretion to use loans, deposits, purchases, assumptions, and contributions to resolve cases and reduce the threat to the insurance fund. However, the FSLIC is required to employ the resolution method that is the least costly to the fund.

There have been two options for resolving the problems of troubled thrift institutions: liquidations or merger/acquisition transactions. While both options involved substantial costs, FSLIC estimates indicated that liquidation was more expensive and, therefore, the option of last resort. For the first nine months of 1988, liquidation costs averaged 65.7 percent of assets while merger/acquisition costs averaged about 58.2 percent. However, congressional studies performed by the General Accounting Office indicated the merger/ acquisition cost advantage had narrowed further by year end 1988. Confusion over the eventual cost of merger notes and future guarantees has raised questions whether liquidation is less costly than merger.

In a merger or acquisition action, a troubled institution is acquired by another, presumably healthier, savings and loan or by investors wanting to enter the industry. The cost of this resolution action is the result of negotiations between the FSLIC and the acquirer. The action usually requires the FSLIC to provide assistance in the form of cash, notes, and various guarantees to help shield the acquirer from the risk of future losses on the institution's assets or from litigation.

The FSLIC's strategy for seriously troubled institutions, particularly those in the Southwest, emphasized using acquisitions or mergers rather than liquidations. By providing assistance in the form of notes and guarantees rather than cash, the FSLIC maximized its limited financial resources. The terms of the notes usually varied, ranging from six months to fifteen years and carrying variable interest rates. The FSLIC made substantial long term financial guarantees in carrying out these transactions, to compensate the acquirers for future losses. In January 1988 the Bush administration abolished the Southwest Plan and its associated use of notes until Congress appropriated more funds.

Something Must Be Done—What Are the Issues?

Even with the CEBA funding, the FSLIC did not have sufficient funds to deal with already bankrupt savings and loans. New sources of funding must be found. During the 1980s, insolvent troubled FSLIC-insured thrifts remained open because the FSLIC did not have the funds or personnel to close them. These institutions were operating under the FHLBB's policy of forbearance. Almost all of these brain-dead thrifts should be closed or merged into healthy institutions.

The cost of implementing the Southwest Plan was significantly greater than the FSLIC anticipated. The FSLIC's forecast reflected in December 31, 1987, financial statements approached $7 billion. However, by December 31, 1988, the cost estimates of Southwest Plan and merger action exceeded $38.6 billion. Final costs will be higher once auditors determine final net worth and asset valuations for the newly formed thrifts. The FSLIC must adjust note guarantee estimates to reflect audited figures as provided in the merger agreements.

There is no consensus about the amount of rescue money required or how it will be funded. This situation results from the divergent interests of the involved parties. Even savings and loan industry groups cannot agree on the magnitude of the problem. Prior funding has come from the industry itself in the form of insurance premiums. Healthy savings and loans, however, cannot continue to mortgage their financial futures by paying premiums and special assessments to bail out bankrupt thrifts. Congress is hesitant to appropriate taxpayer funds, which would greatly increase the already burdensome budget deficit. Other industries, such as banks, and their regulatory funds are apprehensive about the FSLIC predicament and the potential implications.

Recognition of this cancerous problem has fostered numerous governmental agency studies. Studies of the FSLIC dilemma have been conducted by the General Accounting Office, the Department of the Treasury, the National Economic Commission, the Federal Deposit Insurance Corporation, and the banking and savings and loan industries. The final study reports included discussions of many major issues. The Bush administration plan, introduced in February 1989, is expected to lay the foundation for future FSLIC funding and savings and loan industry reform. Significant issues incorporated in the plan are outlined below.

Merger with the FDIC

The Bush administration and other regulatory agencies' plans provide for a merger of the FDIC and the FSLIC. The FDIC has a stronger insurance fund than the FSLIC. Despite the relatively large size and number of bank failures in recent years, additional congressional appropriations have not been required. The bank insurance fund was slightly below $15 billion at year end 1988. With the FSLIC funding shortage estimated to be $50 - $120 billion, the existing FDIC fund would only make a dent in the potential FSLIC liabilities. The FDIC has a special interest in conserving its resources since the banking system has problems of its own. Competitive pressures have forced banks to lower their underwriting standards for approving new loans. Large banks outside the Southwest risk following the fate of failed Texas institutions. Overbuilding and inadequate commercial real estate lending controls provide the potential for a national banking industry slump.

The FDIC and the FSLIC present two models of the deposit insurance function. The FDIC is more independent in its structure and operations. This type of arms length insurance requires coordination with federal and state regulatory and chartering authorities to be effective. The FDIC appears to have been reasonably successful in working out such arrangements with the OCC and the Federal Reserve. For state-chartered nonmember banks, the FDIC has been aided by its role as the federal regulator and supervisor which provide it with more direct control over these institutions.

In contrast, the FSLIC is not independent but is governed by the FHLBB. The FHLBB, which is charged with promoting the availability of funds for home ownership, also regulates the thrift industry and promotes the industry in its role as specialized housing lender. Federal Home Loan District Bank personnel monitor institutions and attempt to resolve problems. Authority and control for all FSLIC operations rests with the FHLBB. Much criticism has been leveled against the FHLBB concerning conflicts of interest. How can an industry promoter judiciously regulate that same industry? Many critics favor splitting the FHLBB duties to separate insurance and regulation of the industry from the chartering of thrifts and the promotion of home financing.

Merger of FSLIC and FDIC funds also has been proposed in the past to facilitate insurance fund recapitalization and administration. Numerous variations of a merger ranging from administrative consolidation to outright dissolution of the FHLBB into the FDIC have been proposed. Under an administrative merger plan, the FDIC umbrella would cover a restructured Bank Board that would only have new charter, examination, and legal responsibility. Benefits would accrue from the potential cost savings generated by overhead consolidation and risk pooling. Standardized closing and liquidation procedures for banks and savings and loans would effect additional cost efficiencies.

A consolidation of the FDIC and FSLIC deposit insurance funds has drawbacks. If the insurance funds are merged, the public could assume that the thrift industry's problems were transferred to the banking system. Overall confidence in the nation's banking system could be adversely affected even if only an administrative merger occurred. At a time when the FDIC should devote all attention to the banking industry, thrift insolvencies would consume all FDIC attention. A merger of the funds is not necessary for the FSLIC to draw on the personnel resources of FDIC or other regulatory agencies. The FDIC could provide temporary contract personnel services as it has done in the past.

Merger proposals for financial or administrative reasons are controversial because of ramifications about the future of the depository institutions system. At present, there are distinctive types of depository institutions: commercial banks, savings institutions, and credit unions. Institutional type similarities have grown due to major deregulatory legislation. But, differences in services remain.

In particular, savings institutions have been distinguished by their commitment to residential housing finance. With regulatory reorganization, thrifts might instead transform themselves into full-service financial operations. Does the nation need an organization of institutions whose principal mission is to finance residential housing? Can we depend on the general marketplace to meet that need? These questions remain to be resolved.

Special Assessments and Risk-Based Assessments

The National Housing Act of 1934 created the FSLIC and a member association assessment mechanism to fund the mandated insurance fund. Although the proposed amount of assessment was widely debated, ranging from 25 to 33 basis points, Congress ultimately authorized an FSLIC premium of 1/12 of 1 percent of deposits, or 8.33 basis points. The original assessment was raised in 1985 with a special levy so that today assessments total 5/24 of 1 percent of deposits, or 20.8 basis points. If the 1933 assessment rate maximum of 33 basis points had been originally implemented, the insurance fund might not be bankrupt today because of the extra funds that would have been generated.

The 1985 special assessment mandates that FSLIC members pay two and one-half times the 1/12 of 1 percent level paid by FDIC-insured banks. Needless to say, savings institutions have voiced heated opposition to the $1.2 billion annual surcharge. Thrifts argue that straddled with such a burden, they cannot compete with banks. Although 90 percent of all FSLIC institutions are solvent, healthy thrifts cannot continue to bear the total burden of bailing out the FSLIC. It is estimated that special assessments reduce the average return on equity of solvent thrifts by 30 to 40 percent. Should economic conditions decline nationally, these so-called healthy thrifts will become the next FSLIC problems. The $1.2 billion annual contribution by healthy thrifts is easily dwarfed by the $50 - $120 billion FSLIC insurance fund problem.

There are two ways to price the FSLIC's insurance risk: adjustment of the insurance premium paid by each thrift, and modification of a thrift's required capitalization level. These adjustments are based upon the riskiness of each thrift's portfolio.

A risk-based premium adjusts the thrift's insurance premium to reflect the expected loss to the FSLIC from the association's risk taking. Under the current system, the FSLIC charges institutions a flat premium rate per dollar of deposits. There is no price placed on the riskiness of individual institutions. Pricing according to risk forces an institution to realize a greater proportion of its risk taking. The major problem with risk-based premiums is determining how and when to judge the risks of a portfolio mix. The advantages of risk-based premiums include reducing the subsidy provided to risky thrifts at the expense of conservative institutions. Proper risk pricing forces thrifts to shoulder their true costs of risk taking. Insurance premiums should produce sufficient income to offset future losses.

Capital requirements are another way to regulate the level of risk undertaken, since capital serves as a cushion against losses. Presently, thrifts face uniform capital requirements, regardless of the risk inherent in their portfolios. Increasing capital requirements as loss probabilities rise protects the insurance fund. Risk-based capital requirements have advantages over risk-based premiums. Potentially large amounts of money do not have to be paid to the FSLIC. Instead, capital market forces will dictate actual funding costs. Institutions perceived by investors to be risky will have to pay more for required reserves.

The State Charter Debate
The savings and loan industry, like the commercial banking system, has a dual federal and state system of chartering new savings and loan institutions. State savings associations are chartered under state statutes and are supervised and examined by state regulators. In contrast, federal thrifts are chartered under federal law and regulated by the FHLBB.

State authorized thrift powers have come under attack because the thrift charters granted by state legislatures are greatly responsible for losses to the FSLIC insurance fund. Up to 86 percent of all FSLIC losses are attributable to state-chartered thrift institutions. Yet they account for less than one half of the savings industry's assets. The majority of the FSLIC's 1988 top one hundred seriously insolvent institutions were state-chartered in Texas.

Congressional leaders have questioned the appropriateness of thrifts to conduct business in a manner not intended by Congress. Why are state-chartered savings associations entitled to more investment latitude than federal associations since both operate under the same federal deposit insurance? Considering the contingent liability, state-chartered thrifts should conduct lending and investment activities in the same manner as federally chartered thrift institutions.

A policy of federal and state charter parity, although a reasonable recommendation, will be difficult if not impossible to implement. State legislative politics will play havoc with any proposal to decrease an individual state's authority. Modifications of bureaucratic structures will be necessary. Despite all the hardships of transition, individual states must bear greater responsibility for state-granted powers. If Texas provided supplemental insurance to cover the additional powers granted to savings associations, the FSLIC's costs to resolve Texas insolvencies would be significantly lower.

The FSLIC insurance fund coverage should be available to state-chartered thrifts only after the sponsoring state provides supplemental risk coverage. The liability of a state-chartered savings and loan association must be borne proportionately with the state's role in granting extra powers.

White Color Crime Enforcement is Needed
The FHLBB had fewer than 750 examiners in 1983 and 1984. Consequently, numerous thrifts were not examined on a timely schedule. No one questions that this fact contributed to the misconduct in numerous institutions that subsequently failed. The Office of Management and Budget (OMB) repeatedly refused to consider FHLBB requests for greater resources during the first half of the decade. That inaction had a severe impact on the Bank Board's enforcement capabilities and significantly contributed to many of the problems now facing the thrift industry. The Reagan administration's budget cuts trimmed the Bank Board's staff, including the examination force, and did not provide necessary pay increases. The annual starting examiner's pay averaged $14,000 in 1980, just when the Bank Board needed skilled personnel the most.

Misconduct and criminality by financial institution insiders has been a major contributing factor to financial institution insolvencies. The federal banking agencies and the Justice Department have not committed adequate resources, established necessary procedures and systems, or adequately shared information among themselves. Substantial progress has been made in interagency coordination and consultation. However, at agency headquarters many serious deficiencies persist and some have worsened. The U.S. government is now confronting a growing long-term epidemic of insider and outsider abuse, misconduct, and criminality in financial institutions. There are large numbers of pending federal criminal investigations of serious bank and thrift fraud.

As of June 30, 1988, there were 7,350 open Federal Bureau of Investigation (FBI) and federal grand jury investigations; 46 percent involved violations where the losses exceeded $100,000 or more. One third of all pending investigations involve financial institutions in California, Texas, and Florida. As of February 1988, the insolvencies of 357 financial institutions were under investigation for criminal misconduct. This was an increase of 161 cases in a two year period. Federal law enforcement authorities expect these numbers to grow as regional economic declines become more prevalent.

Misconduct in financial institutions is often uncovered by regulators or FBI agents only after intensive scrutiny just prior to or after failure. Accordingly, many frauds and abusive acts in open institutions remain undetected unless an area-wide economic crisis or severe mismanagement triggers close scrutiny. Serious misconduct by senior insiders or outsiders was present in the insolvencies of most banks and savings and loans. Insider fraud has caused large losses in healthy and insolvent thrifts during the period from 1984 to the present. At least one third of all commercial bank failures and over three quarters of all savings and loan insolvencies are linked to white collar crime.

Additional federal funding is necessary to stem this tide. The FHLBB requires substantially increased salaries for agency examination, supervisory, and legal staff. Congress must remove the Bank Board's senior staff from the federal appropriations process

(OMB control) since FHLBB operations are fully funded through thrift institution assessments and not tax revenues. Office of Personnel Management should also exempt the FHLBB from current federal budget limitations like all other banking agencies. The banking agencies must substantially increase the number of examiners specifically trained in white collar crime and insider abuse. Training classes should include financial institution and FBI case input.

Banking agencies must increase the number of formal enforcement actions. Formal civil enforcement action should prosecute insiders engaged in unsafe and unsound abusive actions that seriously violate banking regulations. The FSLIC should aggressively collect all outstanding civil money penalties. Delinquent collections should be referred to U.S. attorneys. The regulatory agencies should develop a greater sense of cooperation. Interagency committees need to explore more efficient adjudication of enforcement actions. Uniform rules of practice and procedure merit development. The banking agencies should publicly disclose all formal civil enforcement actions.

The irony about the dismal status of civil enforcement inactivity is that the congressional members who continually gripe about the problem refuse to appropriate the necessary funding. As a result, regulators can do very little except wait for more funds and watch the situation deteriorate. The current state of criminal white collar investigation and enforcement desperately demands correction. There is no reason that the cancer of fraud and misconduct should go undetected until a financial institution is bankrupt. Worse yet, when cases are successfully prosecuted, convicted defendants often receive probation instead of message-sending prison sentences. The criminal justice system levies small fines and probation when the savings and loan industry has suffered billion dollar losses.

Why an Asset Holding Corporation?
The Bush administration has voiced a preference for the establishment of an asset holding corporation to be called the Resolution Trust Corporation. The corporate entity would be a government agency that would take ownership control of the foreclosed and

nonperforming assets of thrift institutions, receiverships, and the FSLIC. The strategic plan would hold the costly real estate obtained through foreclosures for several years until local economies recovered. Eventually the holding corporation would sell the assets at a profit.

A major purported advantage would be the decreased impact on the federal budget deficit. Costs would be amortized over a longer period of time through the use of advanced cost effective financing. A more flexible schedule for the disposition of assets would ensure market stability.

The fundamental problem with this alternative is the probability that the resulting bureaucracy could easily surmount the early FADA debacle. Safeguards to prevent mismanagement and other inefficiencies would be difficult if not impossible to maintain. The sheer magnitude of billions of dollars of depressed real estate provide the possibility of rapid personnel buildup leading to growing pains and disorganization. Professional management personnel requirements would experience the same Federal government restrictions as those presently imposed upon the FHLBB. The questions concerning whether or not employees are Federal government employees would arise. In short, concerns will grow over the corporation's existence as a quasi-government bureaucracy created to manage the real estate problems of the thrift industry. Those inquiries will highlight the more effective use of private contractors and the resulting economic benefits that the private real estate sector can provide.

The Critical Role of Private Industry

As the decade of the 1980s draws to a close, a foggy uneasiness looms over the U.S. real estate industry. The devastated Southwest real estate market conditions have not yet migrated to more distant regions. But as overbuilding continues in the Northeastern, Midwestern, and Western sections of the country, financial institutions will begin to suffer the potential ill effects of overbuilding, market downturn, and prolonged market decline. Unfortunately, nonperforming loan inventories increase slowly and, due to a lack of symptoms, cause no significant concern initially. But as local market declines linger, financial institutions must continue to add staff and balance sheet reserves to be able to carry the foreclosed real estate until better economic times. REO costs have been the cause of multitudes of thrift institution insolvencies and the demise of the FSLIC insurance fund.

Financial institutions, no matter what kind, were never intended to be developers, builders, asset or property managers, or owners of real estate. Although there are some rare exceptions, thrift institutions failed miserably when given far-reaching investment authority under the Garn-St Germain Depository Institutions Act of 1982. The speculative real estate deals of the high-flying Southwest thrifts are responsible for the entire savings industry's downfall. Thrift institutions' primary function must revolve around financial services, not the ownership and management of real estate. Private sector real estate professionals are best suited for that responsibility.

The roles of private sector corporate and individual real estate professionals must greatly expand to meet the challenge of the $50 - $120 billion savings and loan crisis. This problem will not disappear overnight and will require private industry to demand inclusion into the solution. The savings and loan financial crisis presents an unbelievable opportunity for the real estate industry to acquire new business. More than ever before, congressional delegates are eager to hear meaningful private sector recommendations. With the gigantic budget deficit created in the 1980s, Congress must now justify adding even more taxpayer debt. If the real estate community's influence is ineffective, Congress and the Bush administration will solve the crisis without the benefit of real estate sector expertise. The real estate industry and affected subsidiary services must get involved in the thrift crisis solution's early stages and remain active. After all, as taxpayers, real estate professionals will eventually pay their fair share of the cost. The sting can be softened with private enterprise's input.

One of the best ways to participate is to solicit new business from the FSLIC and the FDIC. Opportunities exist for any imaginable real estate related profession or service. Determination and perseverance are definitely needed. Contractors should make contact with FSLIC

Regional Office and receivership staffs. FDIC Regional and Consolidated Offices should be solicited. Potential contractors must determine FSLIC needs and use the techniques described in this book to establish long-lasting relationships. Private industry must understand FSLIC/FDIC receivership problems. Congressional representatives' office staffs should be informed of any roadblocks.

The FSLIC or a merged FSLIC/FDIC liquidation operation will continue to influence real estate market conditions for years to come. The billions of dollars of foreclosed real estate will not be completely bulldozed to the ground; it will not disappear. Cost considerations, which include book value write-downs and good economic sense, make that possibility illogical. Instead, the real estate will require professional operational management to attain the highest value over a period of many years. The opportunity to do business and profit from the FSLIC and the FDIC has never been greater. Private industry must seize that opportunity to provide a stronger financial system for future generations.

APPENDICES

Federal Savings and Loan Insurance Corporation
Operations and Liquidations Division
FSLIC as Receiver, Regional Offices

Eastern Regional Office
1730 Rhode Island Avenue, N.W.
Suite 310
Washington, D.C. 20036
202-955-4530
FAX: 202-955-9369

Eastern Region Area Office
10 South LaSalle Street, Suite 1900
Chicago, IL 60603
312-419-3700
FAX: 312-419-3814

Western Regional Office
523 W. 6th Street, Suite 550
Los Angeles, CA 90014
213-623-7055
FAX: 213-623-9488

Western Regional Area Office
400 S.W. 152nd Street
Seattle, Washington 98166
Mail: P.O. Box 48260
       Seattle, WA 98148
206-241-5505
FAX: 206-243-3926

Central Regional Office
5080 Spectrum Drive
Suite 1000E
Dallas, TX 75248
214-701-2400
FAX: 214-701-3888
     214-701-3999

Federal Asset Disposition Association
FADA Offices

Headquarters
Washington, D.C.
801 17th Street, N.W. Suite 200
Washington, D.C. 20006
202-467-0606
FAX: 202-467-0738

Dallas Office
5080 Spectrum Drive, Suite 1200E
Dallas, TX 75248
214-960-8766
FAX: 214-991-3623

Denver Office
3773 Cherry Creek North Dr., Ste 750
Denver, CO 80209
303-394-4208
FAX: 303-322-3740

Atlanta Office
9000 Central Park, Suite 300
Atlanta, GA 30328
404-393-8400
FAX: 404-399-3152

Los Angeles Office
333 South Hope Street, Suite 3600
Los Angeles, CA 90071
213-687-3232
FAX: 213-972-1237

Federal Home Loan District Banks and Regions

Federal Home Loan Bank of Boston
One Financial Center, 20th Floor
Boston, MA 02110
Mail: P. O. Box 9106 GMF
        Boston, MA 02205-9106
617-542-0150
Connecticut, Maine, Massachusetts, New Hampshire, Rhode Island,
Vermont

Federal Home Loan Bank of New York
One World Trade Center, Floor 103
New York, NY 10048
212-912-4600
New Jersey, New York, Puerto Rico, Virgin Islands

Federal Home Loan Bank of Pittsburgh
One Riverfront Center
Twenty Stanwix Street
Pittsburgh, PA 15222-4893
412-288-3400
Delaware, Pennsylvania, West Virginia

Federal Home Loan Bank of Atlanta
1475 Peachtree Street, N.E.
Atlanta, GA 30309
Mail: P. O. Box 105565
        Atlanta, GA 30348
404-888-8000
Alabama, District of Columbia, Florida, Georgia, Maryland, North
Carolina, South Carolina, Virginia

Federal Home Loan Bank of Dallas
500 E. John Carpenter Freeway
P. O. Box 619026
Dallas/Ft. Worth, TX 75261-9026
214-541-8500
Arkansas, Louisiana, Mississippi, New Mexico, Texas

Federal Home Loan Bank of Topeka
No. 2 Townsite Plaza
120 East 6th Street
Topeka, KS 66603
Mail: P. O. Box 176
       Topeka, KS 66601
913-233-0507
Colorado, Kansas, Nebraska, Oklahoma

Federal Home Loan Bank of Cincinnati
2000 Atrium TWO
221 E. 4th Street
Cincinnati, OH 45202
Mail: P. O. Box 598
       Cincinnati, OH 45201
513-852-7500
Kentucky, Ohio, Tennessee

Federal Home Loan Bank of Indianapolis
1350 Merchants Plaza, South Tower
115 West Washington Street
Indianapolis, IN 46204
Mail: P. O. Box 60
       Indianapolis, IN 46206-0060
317-631-0130
Indiana, Michigan

Federal Home Loan Bank of Chicago
111 East Wacker Drive, Suite 800
Chicago, IL 60601
312-565-5700
Illinois, Wisconsin

Federal Home Loan Bank of Des Moines
907 Walnut Street
Des Moines, IA 50309
515-243-4211
Iowa, Minnesota, Missouri, North Dakota, South Dakota

Federal Home Loan Bank of San Francisco
1 Montgomery Street
Pacific Telesis Center, Suite 400
San Francisco, CA 94104
Mail: P. O. Box 7948
          San Francisco, CA 94120
415-393-1000
Arizona, California, Nevada

Federal Home Loan Bank of Seattle
1501 4th Avenue, 19th Floor
Seattle, WA 98101-1693
206-340-2300
Alaska, Hawaii, Idaho, Montana, Oregon, Utah, Washington,
Wyoming, Guam, Pacific Islands

Federal Deposit Insurance Corporation
Division of Liquidation
Consolidated Offices

Atlanta Region

FDIC, Bossier City Consolidated Office
1325 Barksdale Boulevard
Bossier City, LA 71171-5667
318-742-3290

FDIC, Orlando Consolidated Office
5778 S. Semoran Boulevard
Orlando, FL 32822
407-273-2230

Chicago Region

FDIC, Minneapolis Consolidated Office
501 East Highway 13
Burnsville, MN 55337
612-894-0800

FDIC, Oak Lawn Consolidated Office
900 Oakmont Lane
Westmont, IL 60559
312-789-0300

Dallas Region

FDIC, Addison Consolidated Office
14651 Dallas Parkway, 2nd Floor
Dallas, TX 75230
214-239-3317

FDIC, Houston Consolidated Office
Arena Tower No. 2
7324 Southwest Freeway, Suite 1600
Houston, TX 77074
713-270-6565

FDIC, Midland Consolidated Office
N. Petroleum Building
303 Air Park Drive
Midland, TX 79705
915-685-6400

FDIC, Oklahoma City Consolidated Office
999 NW Grand Boulevard
Oklahoma City, OK 73118
405-842-7441

FDIC, Tulsa Consolidated Office
4606 South Garnett Road
Tulsa, OK 74146
918-627-9000

Kansas City Region

FDIC, Denver Consolidated Office
1125 17th Street, Suite 700
Denver, CO 80202
303-296-4703

FDIC, Kansas City Consolidated Office
Board of Trade Building II
4900 Main Street
Kansas City, MO 64112
816-531-2212

FDIC, Wichita Consolidated Office
1883 W. 21st Street
Wichita, KS 67204
316-838-7111

New York Region

FDIC, Knoxville Consolidated Office
800 S. Gay Street
Knoxville, TN 37909
615-544-4500

FDIC, San Juan Consolidated Office
1607 Ponce de Leon Avenue
Cobian Plaza, Lobby Level
Santurce, PR 00909
809-724-1740

San Francisco Region

FDIC, Costa Mesa Consolidated Office
3347 Michelson Drive, Suite 100
Irvine, CA 92715
714-975-5400

FDIC, San Jose Consolidated Office
2870 Zanker Road
San Jose, CA 95134
408-434-0640

FDIC Division of Liquidation
Regional Offices

FDIC, Atlanta Regional Office
Marquis 1 Building, Suite 1100
245 Peachtree Center Avenue, NE
Atlanta, GA 30303   404-522-1145
Alabama, Florida, Georgia, Louisiana, Mississippi, South Carolina

FDIC, Chicago Regional Office
30 South Wacker Drive, Suite 3200
Chicago, IL 60606   312-207-0200
Illinois, Iowa, Minnesota, North Dakota, South Dakota, Wisconsin

FDIC, Dallas Regional Office
1910 Pacific Avenue, Suite 1700
Dallas, Texas 75201   214-754-0098
Arkansas, Oklahoma, Texas

FDIC, Kansas City Regional Office
Board of Trade Building II, 4900 Main Street
Kansas City, MO 64112   816-531-2212
Kansas, Missouri, Nebraska

FDIC, New York Regional Office
452 5th Avenue, 21st Floor
New York, NY 10018   212-704-1200
Connecticut, Delaware, District of Columbia, Indiana, Kentucky,
Maine, Maryland, Massachusetts, Michigan, New Hampshire, New
Jersey, New York, North Carolina, Ohio, Pennsylvania, Puerto
Rico, Rhode Island, Tennessee, Vermont, Virginia, Virgin Islands,
West Virginia

FDIC, San Francisco Regional Office
25 Ecker Street, Suite 1900
San Francisco, CA 94105   415-546-1810
Alaska, Arizona, California, Colorado, Guam, Hawaii, Idaho,
Montana, Nevada, New Mexico, Oregon, Utah, Washington,
Wyoming

BIBLIOGRAPHY

Federal Deposit Insurance Corporation. *Resolution Costs of Bank Failures.* FDIC Banking Review Paper by John F. Bovenzi and Arthur J. Murton, Vol. 1, No. 1, Fall 1988.

Federal Deposit Insurance Corporation. *Deposit Insurance for the Nineties: Meeting the Challenge.* A Staff Study, January 4, 1989.

Federal Reserve Bank of Dallas. *The Texas Thrift Situation: Implications for the Texas Financial Industry.* Financial Industry Studies Department Report by Genie D. Short and Jeffrey W. Gunther, Dallas, Texas, 1988.

Lockwood, Paul H. *A Guide to the Federal Home Loan Bank System.* Washington, D.C.: FHLB System Publication Corporation, 1987.

State of Texas. *Governor's Task Force on the Savings and Loan Industry Report to William P. Clements, Jr.* Report Executive Order WPC-87-11, January 25, 1988.

U.S. Congressional Record, House Committee on Banking, Finance and Urban Affairs. *Federal Asset Disposition Association: Report of an Inquiry into Its Operations and Performance, 1988.* Staff Report, 100th Cong., April 20, 1988.

U.S. General Accounting Office. *Thrift Industry: The Treasury/ Home Loan Bank Board Plan for FSLIC Recapitalization.* Report No. GAO-GGD-87-46BR, March 3, 1987.

U.S. General Accounting Office. *Thrift Industry: Trends in Thrift Industry Performance: December 1977 through June 1987.* Report No. GAO/GGD-88-87BR, May 17, 1988.

U.S. General Accounting Office. *Thrift Industry: Federal Home Loan Bank Board Advances Program.* Report No. GAO/GGD-88-46BR, March 9, 1988.

U.S. General Accounting Office. *Thrift Industry: Cost to FSLIC of Delaying Action on Insolvent Savings Institutions.* Report No. GAO/GGD-86-122BR, September 9, 1986.

U.S. General Accounting Office, House Committee on Banking, Finance and Urban Affairs. *The Federal Savings and Loan Insurance Corporation's Use of Notes and Assistance Guarantees.* Statement of Frederick D. Wolf, Director of Accounting and Financial Management Division. Report No. GAO/T-AFMD-88-17, 100th Cong., September 8, 1988.

U.S. General Accounting Office. *Thrift Industry: The Management Consignment Program.* Report No. GAO/GGD-87-115BR, September 10, 1987.

U.S. General Accounting Office. *Budget Issues: Information on FDIC and FSLIC Notes Payable.* Report No. GAO/AFMD-88-71FS, August 5, 1988.

U.S. House of Representatives, Committee on Government Operations. *Combating Fraud, Abuse and Misconduct in the Nation's Financial Institutions: Current Federal Efforts are Inadequate.* Report No. 72, 100th Cong., 2nd Sess., October 13, 1988.

U.S. House of Representatives, Committee on Banking, Finance and Urban Affairs. *Hearings on Extinguishment of the FSLIC's Secondary Reserve Fund and Its Impact upon the Nation's FSLIC-Insured Institutions.* Report No. 100-25, 100th Cong., 1st Sess., 1987.

GLOSSARY

Acquirer. Under the Southwest Plan, a healthy thrift institution or corporate merger partner that was the successful bidder in the FHLBB's program for consolidating failing thrifts.

Administrative record. All notices to claimants, Proof(s) of Claim, documentation, and other writings compiled by the special representative that form the basis and rationale for the receiver's determination as to the allowance or disallowance in whole or in part of a claim.

Advisory Council. The Federal Savings and Loan Advisory Council was established by Congress in 1935. It consists of representatives of a broad cross section of the thrift and housing industries, and plays an important role in bringing industry concerns and recommendations to the attention of the Bank Board.

Affected person. A person, corporation, partnership, or other legal entity which has an interest in real or personal property, or is otherwise obligated on a debt secured by real or personal property against which a receiver threatens to take action that may affect, impair, diminish, or terminate such interest.

Amortization. The repayment of a loan calculated so that the principal will be paid in full through monthly payments of principal and interest for a predetermined period of time. Many home mortgages are fully amortized in 15, 20, or 30 years.

Appraisal value. In a business plan, the value of real estate or a real estate-backed asset derived under the guidelines of the FHLBB Memorandum R41C and adjusted if necessary by Federal Home Loan Bank Board instructions.

Asset. Anything owned by an individual or company that has commercial usefulness or value if sold. An asset may be specific property, items, or enforceable claims against others. Loans made by a thrift institution are assets of that institution. Assets also include real estate, equipment, cash, investments in stocks and bonds, and any other resource that can be converted into cash.

Association. An FSLIC-insured savings and loan association or savings bank.

Bank. When lower case in this book, refers to a commercial bank. A commercial bank is an institution that accepts demand deposits and makes commercial loans. When capitalized in this book, refers to one of the 12 Federal Home Loan Banks.

Bank Board. See Federal Home Loan Bank Board.

Banking Act of 1933. The first major banking legislation of the Roosevelt administration, it created the Federal Deposit Insurance Corporation to provide insurance of deposits of member banks, regulated the operation of banks, and limited branch banking. Also known as the Glass-Steagall Act.

Bankruptcy. The legal process in which a person or firm declares inability to pay debts. Any available assets are liquidated and the proceeds are distributed to creditors. A person or firm may be declared bankrupt under one of several chapters of the federal bankruptcy code. Chapter 7, which covers liquidation of the debtor's assets; Chapter 11, which covers reorganization of bankrupt businesses; or Chapter 13, which covers workouts of debts by individuals. Upon a court declaration of bankruptcy, a person or firm surrenders assets to a court-appointed trustee, and is relieved from the payment of previous debts.

Basis point. One basis point equals 1/100th of one percent, or .0001. For example, 50 basis points is equal to 1/2 percent. Basis points are frequently used to describe spreads or changes in yields of interest rates.

Board of directors. The group of persons who make up the governing body of an institution, and are responsible for policy and overall direction of the organization.

Bond. A certificate which is evidence of a debt. The debt is initiated when the issuer sells the bond to the holder for a specific amount of cash. The issuer is obligated to pay the holder of the bond a fixed sum (the bond's face value) at a stated future date and to pay interest (usually twice a year) at a specified rate during the life of the bond. Bonds may be issued by corporations, the Federal government, and by state and local governments as a means of raising funds in the capital markets. Bonds may be issued in registered form, in which the name of the holder is on record with the issuer, or in bearer form, in which the name of the owner is not registered and the bond is payable to whomever bears, or presents, the bond to the issuer for redemption.

Book value. The value of an asset as it appears on the accounting books of an organization. Book value is the initial cost of the asset, less depreciation. Book value may be different from market value, which is the estimated amount the asset would command if sold. Book value also refers to the total value of a company and is computed by adding all assets, then deducting all debts and other liabilities, and deducting the liquidation price of any preferred stock. The book value of a company may be divided by the number of outstanding shares of common stock to get the book value per share of common stock.

Borrower. An individual or institution receiving funds in the form of a loan and obligated to repay the loan, usually with interest. A borrower is called a mortgagor when the loan is secured by real estate.

Breach. A violation of a legal obligation.

Bridge bank. A temporary FDIC failed bank resolution method that allows the FDIC to keep the failed bank operational until a permanent solution can be arranged. If kept operational, a bank can retain much of its value.

Broker. A person who acts as an agent for others in selling or buying funds, securities, real estate, and insurance of other services or projects.

Building and loan association. Another name for a savings and loan association.

Business plan. The written receivership plan describing an asset and its proposed management, disposition, and net realizable value.

Bylaws. The regulations that an institution adopts which set forth duties, limit authority, and establish orderly procedures for conducting business. Bylaws for federal savings institutions are prescribed by the Federal Home Loan Bank Board.

Capital. (1) Funds raised by a business through the sale of stock. (2) Wealth, including money and property, owned, used, or accumulated by a person or a company.

Cease and desist order. A formal demand from the Federal Home Loan Bank Board, other government agency, or court, to a person or institution ordering an immediate halt to a specified activity.

Certificate account. A savings account in which the depositor is issued a certificate that states a fixed amount of funds deposited, the rate of interest to be paid, and the minimum term the certificate must be held in order to collect that interest. Certificate accounts generally pay higher interest than regular passbook or statement accounts. The customer is charged a penalty for premature withdrawal of the funds originally deposited.

Certificate of deposit (CD). The certificate issued to a depositor who opens a certificate account. The certificate is the written document issued by the financial institution as evidence of a deposit. It includes the issuer's promise to return the deposit at a specified future date plus earnings at a specified rate of interest.

Chairman. (1) The highest ranking federal regulator of the savings industry. The chairman is appointed by the President of the United States and is the highest official of the Federal Home Loan Bank Board. (2) The highest ranking executive of a corporation.

Charter. The legal authorization to conduct business, granted by the Federal or state government to a thrift institution or other business or organization.

Claim. The existence of a right to payment or an equitable remedy against an association or a receivership provided, however, it does not include the right to deposit insurance or a Request for Expedited Relief. All receivership claims are submitted in writing in a Proof of Claim.

Claimant. Any person or entity asserting a claim against a failed association or a receiver.

Claims counsel. Legal counsel retained to represent the receiver, as designated by the special representative with the consent of the General Counsel, to perform specified tasks.

Claims procedure. The procedures for the administration and determination of claims filed with the FSLIC as receiver.

Clear title. Title to property that is marketable by virtue of its title being free from demands or claims by other parties and not encumbered in any other manner.

Closing. The consummation of a financial transaction. In mortgage lending, closing is the process of the delivery of a deed; the signing of notes, mortgages, and other loan documents; and the advancing of loaned funds by the lender. All of these transactions normally occur at the same time.

Cloud on the title. An expression meaning that a claim or encumbrance on a property prevents the conveyance of a clear title when the property is sold.

Commercial bank. A financial institution chartered by a state or federal agency that accepts demand deposits, offers commercial loans, and provides other financial services.

Commission. A fee paid to a person for conducting a business transaction or performing a service. A commission is usually based on a percentage of the total transaction.

Comptroller of the Currency. A federal office created by Congress in 1863 as part of the national banking system. The Comptroller of the Currency charters and regulates national banks.

Conservator. An official placed in charge of a troubled savings institution by the Federal Home Loan Bank Board to protect and preserve the assets of the institution while more permanent measures for dealing with the institution are worked out.

Conversion. In the financial services industry, the term refers to a change of ownership of a thrift institution from mutual to stock form (or vice versa), or a change of charter from state to federal (or vice versa).

Cost approach to value. An approximation of the market value of improved real estate measured as the cost of reproduction or replacement.

Cost basis. The original price of an asset, normally the purchase price or the appraised value of the asset at the time of acquisition.

Cost of capital. All debt and equity costs, actual or imputed, associated with the advancement of funds to operate, maintain, improve, or complete an asset of a receivership for the purpose of liquidation. For purposes of the calculation of net realizable value of an asset, cost of capital is recognized through the discounting of expected costs and revenues to present value.

Cost of funds. The interest paid or accrued on savings, advances from a Federal Home Loan Bank, or on other funds borrowed by a thrift institution, expressed as a percent of the average total savings and borrowings during a given accounting period.

Credit bureau. An agency that collects and distributes credit history information of individuals and businesses.

Credit rating. An estimate of the likelihood that a borrower will repay a loan on time. This measure of credit worthiness is based on the borrower's present financial condition, past credit history, integrity, and experience.

Credit union. A cooperative organization chartered by state or Federal government that accepts savings from its members and makes low interest loans to its members. Credit unions are normally formed among members who are employed by the same company or are members of the same organization.

Creditor. A party to whom money is owed by another. In a receivership, a depositor who exceeds $100,000 in deposits or a vendor/contractor who remains unpaid after providing goods and services before an FSLIC takeover.

Currency. Coins and paper money, which circulate as a legal medium of exchange.

Deed in lieu of foreclosure. The transfer of title to real property from a delinquent mortgagor to the mortgagee, given to satisfy the obligation of repaying the balance due on the defaulted loan and thus preventing foreclosure.

Deed of trust. A deed that establishes a trust. It is used in some loan transactions in place of a mortgage. In a trust deed the property on which money has been lent is conveyed as collateral to a trustee, who holds it in trust for the benefit of the holder or holders of the loan notes. The trust deed states the authority of the trustee and any conditions which govern the actions of the trustee in dealing with the property. These include the condition that the trustee shall reconvey the title of the property to the buyer when the debt has been repaid. The trustee also has power to sell the property and pay the debt in the event of a default of the debtor.

Deficiency judgment. A court order that declares the property securing a debt to be worth less than the amount of outstanding debt. It authorizes the collection from the debtor of the part of the debt remaining unsatisfied after foreclosure and sale of collateral.

De novo. New, fresh, just beginning. A de novo thrift institution is a newly chartered institution. De novo branching refers to opening a new branch office as opposed to buying an existing branch or acquiring branches through a merger of institutions.

Deposit. (1) The placement of funds into an account at an institution in order to increase the credit balance of the account. (2) That which is deposited. (3) A sum of money given to assure the future purchase of something. (4) A portion of the purchase price given as earnest money, or a down payment, by the buyer to the seller.

Depositor. A person or entity that places funds in an account at a financial institution.

Depository institution. A financial intermediary that accepts savings or demand deposits from the general public.

Depository Institutions Deregulation Committee (DIDC). Created under the Depository Institutions Deregulation and Monetary Control Act of 1980. The committee is made up of the principal federal financial regulators. It was responsible for implementing the orderly phaseout and ultimate elimination of federally imposed ceilings on savings deposit interest rates by March 31, 1986.

Deposit payoff. An FDIC failed bank resolution method whereby the bank is closed by the chartering authority and the FDIC is appointed receiver. The FDIC pays all depositors the full amount of their insured claims.

Direct investment. Investment by thrift institutions directly in the equity of such ventures as real estate development and business firms, as opposed to thrifts' traditional debt investment. With direct investment, a thrift institution actually owns all or a portion of a venture, rather than simply lending money to finance the venture. Direct investments can be more profitable— and more risky—than debt investments.

Director. The Director (or acting Director) of the Office of the Federal Savings and Loan Insurance Corporation.

Direct selling costs. All direct costs including, but not limited to, brokers fees and commissions, settlement attorney fees, advertising expenses, title fees, survey fees, and other miscellaneous fees incurred as the result of the final disposition of an asset by a receivership.

Discount rate. As used by an appraiser, it is a blended rate of (1) a market rate of interest available to builder/developers for borrowed funds; (2) a rate of return for investors of equity funds; and (3) an entrepreneurial rate of return expected by the builder/developer. Entrepreneurial profit can be treated as a deduction from fair market value or as a component of the blended discount rate. As used by the asset manager in calculation of NRV, the discount rate is the Treasury bill rate for the estimated holding period.

Disintermediation. The movement of funds from one investment vehicle to another; for example, the withdrawal of funds from depository institutions for the purpose of investing the same funds in higher yielding money market instruments.

District Banks. Refers to each of the 12 Federal Home Loan Banks or the 12 Federal Reserve System Banks.

Diversification. The participation by a firm in the production or sale of widely divergent kinds of goods or services. Diversification permits the company to minimize the impact on overall revenue of business fluctuations in a single market, single product, or service line.

Dual-banking system. Refers to the emergence of two systems—state and federal—which charter and regulate banks and savings institutions.

Dumping. The sale of any asset or number of assets that causes a decline in market value of comparable assets in the marketplace.

Earnest money. A sum of money given to bind an agreement, such as the sale of real estate. Earnest money is forfeited by the donor if he or she fails to carry out the terms of the contract or agreement.

Earnest money contract. See purchase agreement.

Encumber. To burden real estate with a lien or a charge such as a mortgage.

Encumbrance. A claim attached to real property, such as a lien, mortgage, or unpaid taxes.

Equitable right of redemption. A right under state law of a defaulted borrower to redeem his or her property by paying in full the outstanding mortgage debt up to the date of the mortgage foreclosure sale.

Equity. In real estate, equity is the difference between the fair market value of a property and the amount of any mortgage debt, or liens against the property, still outstanding. In business, the excess of a firm's assets over its liabilities. The term is also used to refer to the ownership interest of stockholders in a company, and to the value of the investments raised by the stock offerings.

Escrow. A written agreement under which documents, funds, or other property being transferred from one party to another are placed with a third person or entity, usually a trust company, acting as custodian. The custodian completes the transfer to the second party only upon the fulfillment of certain specified conditions.

Eurobond. A bond issued for release by a U.S. or other non-European company or government for sale in Western Europe. In that market, corporations and governments normally issue medium-term securities with maturities of 10 to 15 years.

Examination. A supervisory examination is a detailed review of a savings association's operations and books made by a supervisory authority such as the Federal Home Loan Bank Board.

Examiner. An individual employed by a federal or state supervisory agency to conduct detailed reviews of the operation of savings institutions in order to determine if the institutions are meeting the requirements of federal law and regulation.

Exclusive listing. A written contract giving one agent the exclusive right to sell or rent a property during a stated period of time.

Exclusive right to sell. Same as exclusive listing, except that the owner agrees in writing to pay the full commission to the broker even if the owner himself sells or rents the property.

FADA. See Federal Asset Disposition Association.

Fair market value. The price at which property would be transferred from a willing seller to a willing buyer, each of whom has a reasonable knowledge of all pertinent facts concerning the property in question and similar properties on the market, and neither being under any compulsion to buy or sell.

Farmers Home Administration (FmHA). A Federal government agency that finances and insures loans to farmers and other qualified borrowers for rural housing and other purposes.

FDIC. See Federal Deposit Insurance Corporation.

Federal Asset Disposition Association (FADA). A federal savings and loan association chartered by the Federal Home Loan Bank Board in November 1985. Although the FADA may accept deposits, it was chartered for the sole purpose of liquidating and disposing of assets of failed savings institutions acquired by the Federal Savings and Loan Insurance Corporation (FSLIC) in its role as receiver. Since it was chartered under Section 406 of the National Housing Act, the FADA is informally known as a "406 corporation."

Federal association. A savings and loan, building and loan, or homestead association or savings bank chartered by the Federal Home Loan Bank Board.

Federal Deposit Insurance Corporation (FDIC). A government corporation that insures deposits in member commercial banks and some mutual savings banks.

Federal Home Loan Bank (FHLB). One of the 12 regional Banks of the Federal Home Loan Bank System. The Banks were established to extend loans, provide various services, and examine and supervise member institutions, including savings and loan associations and savings banks.

Federal Home Loan Bank Board (FHLBB). An independent agency in the executive branch of the Federal government that governs the Federal Home Loan Bank System, the Federal Savings and Loan Insurance Corporation, and the Federal Home Loan Mortgage Corporation. The agency charters federal savings institutions and regulates all institutions that are members of the system or are insured by the FSLIC.

Federal Home Loan Bank Board Memorandum. The Bank Board publishes several memorandum series that include interpretations of regulations, instructions on compliance, and opinions. The primary series are the R, T, SP, AB, and PA memos.

Federal Home Loan Bank System. The Federal Home Loan Bank Board, the 12 regional Federal Home Loan Banks, the member savings and loan associations, savings banks, and life insurance companies all make up the FHLB System. The primary purpose of the System is to serve as a central credit facility for member institutions.

Federally chartered association. Federal savings associations that are chartered under the provisions of the Home Owners Loan Act of 1933, and are subject to the supervision of the Federal Home Loan Bank Board. Federal savings associations are required by law to have their savings accounts insured by the FSLIC and to be members of a Federal Home Loan Bank.

Federal Open Market Committee (FOMC). A 12 member committee consisting of the seven members of the Federal Reserve Board and five of the 12 Federal Reserve Bank presidents. The president of the Federal Reserve Bank of New York is a permanent member while the other Federal Reserve presidents serve on a rotating basis. The committee sets objectives for growth of money and credit that are implemented through purchases and sales of U.S. Government securities in the open market. The FOMC also establishes policy relating to Federal Reserve System operations in the foreign exchange markets.

Federal Reserve System. Consists of the Federal Reserve Board, the 12 regional Federal Reserve Banks, federally chartered commercial banks, and state-chartered commercial banks that elect to be members. The Federal Reserve System serves as a central credit facility for member commercial banks, and controls the nation's money supply.

Federal Savings and Loan Insurance Corporation (FSLIC). A government corporation created by Congress and controlled by the Federal Home Loan Bank Board to insure deposits in member savings institutions up to $100,000 per individual per account.

Federal savings association. A savings association chartered and regulated by the Federal Home Loan Bank Board.

FDIC. See Federal Deposit Insurance Corporation.

FHLB. See Federal Home Loan Bank.

FHLBB. See Federal Home Loan Bank Board.

Fiduciary. Someone who is entrusted with the care of another person's money, property, or other items of value.

Financial Accounting Standards Board (FASB). A seven member body that establishes rules governing accounting practices throughout the U.S. Founded in 1972, FASB is under the direction of the Financial Accounting Foundation, a private sector trust.

Financial institution. A corporation chartered for the purpose of dealing primarily with money, such as deposits, investments, and loans, rather than goods or services.

Financial intermediary. A financial institution that accepts money from savers or investors and loans those funds to borrowers, thus providing a link between those seeking earnings on their funds and those seeking credit. Financial intermediaries include savings and loan associations, building and loan associations, savings banks, commercial banks, life insurance companies, credit unions, and investment companies.

Financial statements. Reports that summarize a firm's accounting data and indicate its financial condition. The four basic financial statements are the balance sheet, income statement, statement of retained earnings, and statement of changes in financial position.

Forbearance. The act of surrendering the right to enforce a valid claim in return for a binding promise to perform a specified act. In the thrift industry, forbearance usually refers to the Bank Board refraining from taking enforcement action against a thrift institution as long as certain conditions are met.

Foreclosure. A legal proceeding by which a mortgage lender may claim title to a mortgaged property if the borrower fails to repay the loan.

FSLIC. See Federal Savings and Loan Insurance Corporation.

Full faith and credit. A pledge of a government to commit its general taxing power to raise funds for payment of obligations.

GAAP. See Generally Accepted Accounting Principles.

General contractor. A party that performs or supervises the construction or development of a property pursuant to the terms of a primary contract with the property owner. The general contractor may use its own employees to perform the work and the services of other contractors called subcontractors.

General Counsel. The legal counsel for the Federal Home Loan Bank Board or an attorney(s) in the Office of General Counsel.

General partner. A co-owner(s) of a business who is liable for all debts and other obligations of the venture as well as for the management and operation of the partnership. A general partner can have control of the business and can take actions that are binding on the other partners.

General reserves. The funds that are set aside by a financial institution for the sole purpose of covering possible losses.

Generally Accepted Accounting Principles (GAAP). Accounting rules and procedures adopted by the accounting profession to facilitate uniformity in preparing financial statements.

Glass-Steagall Act. See Banking Act of 1933.

Gross National Product (GNP). The most comprehensive measure of a nation's total output of goods and services. It consists of the total retail market value of all items and services produced in a country during a specified period.

Guarantor. An individual, institution, or other entity that guarantees to repay a debt if the borrower defaults.

Highest and best use. An appraisal and zoning concept that evaluates all the possible, permissible, and profitable uses of a property to determine the use that will provide the owner with the highest net return on investment in the property, consistent with existing, neighboring land uses.

Historic cost. The dollar amount of the assets on the books of the association as of a specific date and before any loss allowance reserve taken by the association. Historic cost for mortgages and similar loans is the original loan commitment less principal payments received up to the specific date net of any unamortized premiums, discounts, fees, loans-in-process, or unfunded commitments.

Holding period. The period between acquisition of an asset from the association by the receivership through disposition, including the time required to obtain marketable title.

Holding revenues and costs. All estimated revenues and costs of maintaining an asset between the date of acquisition and final disposition.

Home Owners' Loan Corporation (HOLC). A federally chartered corporation established in 1933 and administered by the Federal Home Loan Bank Board to refinance mortgages of economically distressed homeowners. The HOLC legally expired in 1954.

Income approach to value. The process of estimating the market value of a property by comparing the net rental income the property would produce over its remaining effective life with the yields that could be obtained from other kinds of investments of comparable risk.

Income capital certificate (ICC). An instrument developed by the Federal Savings and Loan Insurance Corporation to provide assistance to troubled thrift institutions. Under the program, the thrift issues ICCs to the FSLIC in return for cash or the FSLIC's promissory notes. The thrift may count outstanding ICCs as part of its net worth. As the institution regains financial health, the ICCs are retired.

Income property. Real estate owned or operated to produce revenue.

Income statement. A financial statement that contains a summary of a business's financial operations for a specific period of time. It shows the net profit or loss for the period by stating the company's revenues and expenses.

Indemnity. (1) Payment for damage, a guarantee against losses. (2) A bond protecting the insured against losses caused by others failing to fulfill their obligations. (3) The granting of exemption from prosecution. (4) An option to buy or sell a specific quantity of stock at a stated price within a given period of time.

Inflation. An economic condition marked by a decrease in the purchasing power of the dollar and a general rise in prices.

Insider. An individual who by virtue of his or her employment or other close relationship has information on the financial status of a firm or a particular transaction before that information is available to the general public.

Insolvency. The inability to pay one's debts as they come due. Even though the total assets of an organization may exceed its total liabilities, the entity is insolvent if the asset cannot be converted into cash to meet the current obligations.

Insolvent. The state of being unable to pay debts when demanded by creditors at maturity.

Institutional lender. A financial institution or mortgage lender that invests its own capital and other funds under its management in real estate mortgages. Examples include savings and loan associations, savings banks, commercial banks, life insurance companies, and pension and trust funds.

Insured deposit transfer. An FDIC failed bank resolution method whereby only the insured deposits and secured liabilities are transferred to another institution. Uninsured and secured liabilities remain with the FDIC as receiver.

Intangible asset. An asset that has no substance or physical properties. Items of intellectual property. Intangible assets include goodwill, patent rights, franchises, trademarks, and copyrights.

Intermediation. The process carried out by a financial institution serving as a link, or intermediary, between borrowers and savers. Savers deposit funds in the institution, which lends those funds to home buyers and other borrowers.

Joint account. A savings account in the names of two or more people. Joint accounts may carry rights of survivorship or may be established on a tenants-in-common basis without such rights.

Joint venture. A commercial project, usually of a limited duration or for a specific accomplishment, undertaken by two or more persons or companies.

Judgment lien. A court order placing a claim on property of a debtor making the property security for payment of the debt. When applied to personal property, it is known as an attachment.

Judicial foreclosure. A type of foreclosure proceeding used in some states that is handled as a civil lawsuit and conducted under the auspices of a court.

Junk bonds. Wall Street slang for bonds listed at below investment grade (below the top four ratings) by agencies that rate bonds. Such bonds are frequently unsecured or thinly backed by company assets, and carry a relatively high level of risk for investors. The bonds must pay high yields, commonly 3 to 4 percent above high-grade corporate bonds. Some junk bonds are issued by those seeking to raise funds to finance their buying of stock and takeover of corporations, the assets of which are liquidated to pay for redemption of the bonds.

Land flip. A technique to artificially increase the book value of a parcel of land. The land is sold several times in quick succession among persons acting in concert, with the price increasing each time the land is sold. In a land flip, multiple sales of the same property can occur within a few days.

Letter of credit. A document issued by a financial institution on behalf of a buyer stating the amount of credit the buyer has available. The institution will honor drafts up to that amount written by the buyer. It gives the buyer the prestige and financial backing of the issuing institution and satisfies the seller requirements in completing the transaction. The accepting institution has a prior agreement as to how the buyer will pay for the drafts as they are presented.

Letter of intent. A written document usually in letter form that carefully, yet simply, defines basic terms and conditions for a proposed asset purchase.

Lien. A claim by one person on the property of another person as security for the payment of a debt.

Limited partnership. A partnership that consists of at least one general partner who is fully personally liable for the debts of the partnership, and one or more limited partners who are each liable only for the amount of their own investment.

Line of credit. A pre-established loan authorization with a specified borrowing limit extended by a lending institution to an individual or business based on credit worthiness. A line of credit allows borrowers to obtain a number of loans without reapplying each time as long as the total of borrowed funds does not exceed the credit limit.

Liquid assets. The total amount of funds that are in the form of cash or can quickly be converted to cash. These include (1) cash; (2) demand deposits; (3) time and savings deposits; and (4) investments capable of being quickly converted into cash without significant loss, either through their sale or through the scheduled return of principal at the end of a short time remaining to maturity.

Liquidation. The process of terminating a business, including selling assets to obtain cash and using the cash to discharge liabilities.

Listing. A written authorization by the owner to sell or lease real property.

Litigation. The act of engaging in and proceeding with a lawsuit.

Loan participation. (1) The buying of portions of outstanding loans by investors, who then participate on a pro rata basis in collecting interest and principal payments. (2) The sharing by two or more lenders in the ownership of a loan or package of loans.

Loan pool. A pool of performing or nonperforming loans similar in type (i.e., mortgage, construction, consumer, etc.), dollar value, and yield.

Loan portfolio. The total of all the loans that a financial institution, or other lender, holds at a given time.

Loan servicing. The act performed to collect and process loan payments during the life of a loan. They include billing the borrower; collecting payments of principal, interest, and payments into an escrow account; disbursing funds from the escrow account to pay taxes and insurance premiums; and forwarding funds to an investor if the loan has been sold in the secondary market.

Loan workout. A series of steps taken by a lender with a borrower to resolve the problem of delinquent loan payments.

Loss allowance reserve. The estimated uncollectible portion of an asset as determined by the association.

MACRO. A rating system by which examiners evaluate the financial condition of savings institutions. MACRO is an acronym for the five elements that are evaluated. Management, Asset quality, Capital adequacy, Risk management, and Operating results. Based on the examiner's evaluation of these elements, each savings institution examined by the Federal Home Loan Bank System is assigned a rating on a scale from one to five. Rating 1 indicates a strong performance and Rating 5 is considered unsatisfactory.

Marketable title. Title to property that is free of defects and that will legally be accepted without objection. Also known as perfect title, clear title, and good title.

Market data approach to value. The estimation of a property's market value by comparing it with similar properties in the general area that have sold recently under comparable conditions.

Market value. The highest price a property will bring in a competitive and open market. The price which an owner is prepared to accept to sell property and a buyer is willing to pay.

Material asset. Any asset (tangible or intangible) with a net takeover value which is the lesser of one percent of portfolio value or $500,000.

Mechanic's lien. A legal, enforceable claim for payment of a person who has performed work or supplied materials used in the construction or repair of a building. The building and land is attached as security for payment of the claim. Mechanic's liens are permitted by the laws of most states. Also called a materialmen's lien.

Members. (1) All the savers and borrowers in a mutual savings institution who have the right to elect directors, amend the bylaws, and approve any basic corporate change, policy, or organization. They posses most of the rights of ownership that stockholders have in a stock corporation, except the right to share in profits. (2) Financial institutions that belong to the Federal Home Loan Bank System and join one of the 12 Federal Home Loan Banks. (3) The appointed officials, other than the Chairman, who serve on the Federal Home Loan Bank Board.

Memorandum. See Federal Home Loan Bank Board memorandum.

Merger. The combining of two or more savings institutions or other entities through one acquiring the assets and liabilities of the other(s). The acquired institutions lose their corporate identity and are absorbed into the surviving institution.

Money market fund. The combined money of many individuals that is jointly invested in high yield financial instruments including U.S. government securities, certificates of deposit, and commercial paper. A money market fund is a mutual fund which strives to make a profit by buying and selling various forms of money rather than buying and selling shares of ownership in corporations.

Mortgage. A legal document by which real property is pledged as security for the repayment of a loan. The pledge is cancelled when the debt is paid in full.

Mortgage-backed bonds. Bonds that are secured by mortgages. Unlike mortgage-backed pass-through securities, mortgage-backed bonds do not convey ownership of any portion of the underlying pool of mortgages. However, mortgage-backed bonds do offer a more predictable maturity and thus offer a form of call protection.

Mortgage-backed pass-through securities. Securities that convey ownership of a fractional part of each mortgage in a pool of mortgages backing the securities. Mortgage payments are sent to the issuer of the securities and then passed through to those who bought the securities. Each security owner shares proportionally the interest and principal payments generated by the underlying pool of mortgages.

Mortgage loan. An advance of funds from a lender, called the mortgagee, to a borrower, called the mortgagor, secured by real property and evidenced by a document called a mortgage. The mortgage sets forth the conditions of the loan, the manner and duration of repayment, and the mortgagee's right to repossess the pledged property if the mortgagor fails to repay any portion of principal and interest.

Mortgage portfolio. The total of all mortgage loans held by a lender or investor.

Mortgagee. The institution, group, or individual that lends money secured by pledged real estate; the lender.

Mortgagor. The owner of real estate who pledges the property as security for the repayment of a debt; the borrower.

Mutual association. A savings association that is owned and controlled solely by its savers and borrowers, who are called members. A mutual association does not issue capital stock, and its members do not share in profits of the association. They do exercise other ownership rights such as the right to elect directors of the association. See stock association.

Mutual fund. A financial corporation that sells shares of its own stock and invests the funds thus raised in the stock and securities of other corporations or government securities. Dividends paid to shareholders are based on the earnings of the securities held by the fund, minus operating expenses. A mutual fund pools the funds of many investors and provides professional management in investing those funds. Also called an open-end investment company.

Mutual savings bank. A financial institution chartered by state or Federal government to: (1) provide a safe place for individuals to save and (2) invest those savings in mortgages loans, stocks, bonds, and other securities. Most mutual savings banks are located in the Northeast, and are owned by their depositors and borrowers. A mutual savings bank does not issue capital stock. Profits are distributed to the owner/customers in proportion to the business they do with the institution.

National Council of Savings Institutions. A trade organization formed by the November 1, 1983, merger of the National Savings and Loan League and the National Association of Mutual Savings Banks.

National Credit Union Administration (NCUA). The federal agency that supervises, charters, and insures federal credit unions. NCUA also insures state-chartered credit unions that apply and qualify for insurance. In addition, the NCUA operates a central credit facility for member credit unions.

Neighborhood Housing Services (NHS) programs. Programs aimed at halting the further decline of neighborhoods that have begun to deteriorate. They are based on a partnership of community residents, lenders, and local government. NHS is administered by the Neighborhood Reinvestment Corporation.

Neighborhood Reinvestment Corporation. Created by the Housing and Community Development Act of 1978 to help establish locally run self-help coalitions of business leaders, residents, and local government officials, called Neighborhood Housing Services (NHS) programs. They encourage communities to revitalize depressed urban neighborhoods and thus make home financing more attractive in these areas.

Net income. Gross income less expenses, including taxes and insurance, but before depreciation, additions to reserves, or distribution of earnings.

Net realizable value (NRV). The present value, as of the takeover date, of the estimated cash proceeds, adjusted by the present values of revenues and expenses anticipated throughout the holding period, from the liquidation of an asset on the most probable date of sale or disposition pursuant to the business plan for such asset.

Net takeover value (NTV). Historic cost of an asset less the association loss allowance reserve. The net takeover value becomes the receivership book value at the date of takeover and will be written down to net realizable value if NRV is less than the net takeover value. If net realizable value is greater than the net takeover value, the net takeover value will be written up to NRV.

Net savings inflow. The change during a given period of an institution's total savings account liability, determined by adding all deposits and subtracting all withdrawals. Also referred to as net savings gain or net savings receipts. When interest credited to accounts during the period is excluded, the resulting total is referred to as net new savings.

Net worth. The value in dollars of all assets less all liabilities. In the savings and loan industry net worth is also expressed as a percent of assets. It is computed by subtracting liabilities from assets and dividing that number by assets.

Net worth certificates. Instruments authorized by the Garn-St Germain Depository Institutions Act of 1982, to assist thrift institutions in meeting minimum regulatory net worth requirements. A thrift participating in the program issues net worth certificates to the FSLIC in return for the FSLIC's promissory notes. The notes may be counted as part of the institution's net worth. As the institution regains financial health, it begins to redeem the net worth certificates by returning the FSLIC's promissory notes.

Non-bank bank. A financial institution which does not meet the legal definition of a commercial bank, and thus avoids the prohibition against branching across state lines. It avoids being classified as a commercial bank by not engaging in one of the two lines of business that define commercial banks: demand deposits or commercial loans.

Nondepository financial institution. A company that deals in financial instruments but does not accept deposits. Examples are insurance companies and brokerage firms.

Non-recourse loan. A type of loan in which the only remedy available to the lender in the event of the borrower's default is to foreclose on the collateral. The borrower is not personally liable for repayment.

NRV. See net realizable value.

Offer to purchase. See purchase agreement.

Office of General Counsel (OGC). The legal counsel to the Federal Home Loan Bank Board.

Open bank assistance. An FDIC failed bank resolution transaction whereby prior to the failing bank being closed, private investors agree to inject new capital. The FDIC provides assistance to cover the bank's negative net worth. All depositors and some general creditors are protected against loss.

Operating budget. A detailed projection of all estimated income and expenses during a given future period.

Originate a loan. To make or issue a loan. The process whereby a lender qualifies a borrower, appraises the collateral, processes all documents, advances funds, and places the loan on the books.

Origination fee. Charge imposed by a lender for the evaluation, preparation, and processing of loan applications.

Other Real Estate (ORE). The banking industry's term for foreclosed real estate. This terminology differs from the savings and loan classification of real estate owned (REO).

Participation. (1) Ownership by two or more lenders or investors of all or a portion of a single mortgage or a package of mortgages. (2) The cooperative origination by two or more lenders of a single (usually large) mortgage loan.

Participation loan. A loan made or owned by more than one lender. The joint investors share profits and losses in proportion to how much of the loan each owns.

Partnership. A form of business organization in which two or more persons join in a business or commercial enterprise, sharing profits, risks, and losses according to the terms set forth in their partnership contract.

Passbook account. A savings account that normally does not require a minimum balance, a minimum term, a specified frequency of deposits, or a notice or penalty for withdrawals. The actual passbook, in which transactions are recorded, is rapidly being replaced by a monthly statement mailed to the depositor.

Pass-through security. A security granting the holder an interest in a pool of mortgages. Payments of principal and interest on the underlying mortgages are passed through to the holder of the security.

Period of redemption. The period of time during which a mortgagor may reclaim the title and possession of his property by paying the debt the property secures.

Permanent lender. A lender that provides long-term financing for projects after construction has been completed.

Permanent loan. A long-term loan of not less than ten years that is fully amortized and made to purchase, rather than to construct, real property.

Personal loan. An unsecured loan usually made for the purpose of debt consolidation, vacation, or the purchase of durable goods. Also called a signature loan.

Personal property. (1) Any property that is not real property. (2) While state laws vary on the definition of state property, it is generally thought of as the moveable items that a person owns. They can be tangible, such as furniture and other merchandise, or intangible, such as stocks and bonds.

Pledged loan. A mortgage loan that has been identified and set aside as security for borrowing by the holder of the mortgage, particularly a loan that has been pledged as security for an advance from a Federal Home Loan Bank.

Point. An amount equal to one percent of the principal amount of an investment or a loan. Points are a one time charge assessed at closing by the lender to increase the lender's earnings on mortgage loans.

Ponzi scheme. An operation intended to defraud investors in which no new wealth is produced, and creditors are paid off by borrowing ever larger amounts from new investors.

Pool. A large group of mortgages which back a mortgage security.

Portfolio. All of the income-producing assets held by an individual or institution, such as the income-earning securities and mortgage loans of a savings institution.

Power of attorney. A document that authorizes one person to legally act as the agent for, or in place of, another person in performing various actions under specified conditions. Full power may be granted, or authority may be limited to certain functions.

Premium. (1) The amount, often stated as a percentage, paid in addition to the face value of a note or bond. (2) A fee charged for the granting of a loan. (3) The price paid for an insurance contract. (4) A product given free or sold at discount, offered as an inducement to the public to open or add to a savings account, or to purchase other specified products or services.

Present value cost. The cost in currently valued dollars of funds to be expended over a period of time, usually a number of years, less the net of any funds to be repaid. It is adjusted to compensate for the loss or gain of the opportunity to invest the funds rather than spend them, that is for the dollars' estimated earning potential in alternative uses. For example, the present value cost is reduced by the amount of income the funds are expected to earn until they are disbursed, and increased to compensate for the loss of earnings thereafter, or until such time as the funds are repaid. Present value cost is used by the FSLIC to estimate the impact on the insurance fund of alternative solutions to troubled thrift institutions.

Principal. (1) The capital sum of a loan. The amount of borrowed funds to be repaid. (2) An individual or firm buying or selling for his (her/its) own account.

Principal supervisory agent (PSA). An officer of a Federal Home Loan Bank, normally the Bank's president, who is designated by the Federal Home Loan Bank Board as the chief enforcement officer of federal law and Bank Board regulation for the savings institutions in the Bank's district.

Private enterprise. An economy in which the production of goods and services is carried out by businesses owned and operated by people risking their investment of capital and/or labor in the hope of making a profit.

Private sector. That portion of the economy composed of businesses and households, and excluding government.

Promissory note. A written promise to pay a stipulated sum of money to a specified party under conditions mutually agreed upon. Also called a note, promise, or bond.

Proof of claim. The form specified by the Director of the FSLIC, with the concurrence of the General Counsel, upon which a claim of a creditor of a failed thrift shall be submitted in writing to a receivership.

Purchase agreement. A signed document stating the purchaser's agreement to buy and the seller's agreement to sell a specified property under stated terms and conditions, also known as an earnest money contract or offer to purchase.

Purchase and assumption (P&A). An FDIC failed bank resolution transaction whereby a buyer purchases all or some of the failed bank's assets and assumes its deposits and certain liabilities. All depositors, insured and uninsured, receive full payment on their claims.

Purchase money mortgage. A mortgage given to the seller, with the mortgage constituting all or part of the compensation received for the sale of property. Such a mortgage is used when the seller is also the lender.

Rate intermediation. Borrowing funds at short-term interest rates and lending the funds at longer term fixed rates.

Rate-sensitive. Describes a deposit account or security investment for which changes in its interest rate produce wide fluctuations in its supply and/or demand.

Real estate investment trust (REIT). An investment vehicle established for the benefit of a group of real estate investors. A REIT is an unincorporated trust or association, managed by one or more trustees who hold title to the assets of the trust and control its acquisitions and investments. Real estate investments commonly include office buildings, apartment houses, and shopping centers. A REIT can provide significant income tax benefits.

Real estate owned (REO). Real estate owned by a savings institution as the result of default by borrowers and subsequent foreclosure by the institution.

Real property. All immovable property, such as land and the buildings or other objects permanently affixed to the land.

Receiver. The FSLIC or other contracting agent acting for the FSLIC, appointed for the purpose of liquidating any association through a legal receivership; such appointment may be by any of the methods prescribed by law and regulation to effect such appointment.

Receivership. A legal entity, limited in scope and time, established for the purpose of liquidating the assets of a defaulted savings and loan association.

Receivership book value (RBV). Net takeover value written up or down to net realizable value.

Receivership date. The date and time at which the receiver assumed possession and control of the association.

Recourse. (1) The right of a holder in due course to demand payment from the maker or endorser of a negotiable instrument, or from prior endorsers if the instrument is dishonored by the maker. (2) In the secondary mortgage market, recourse refers to a provision in the sales contract by which a mortgage seller agrees to buy back the loan if default and foreclosure occur.

Regulation. (1) A rule adopted by the Federal Home Loan Bank Board. (2) The act or process of governing or regulating.

Regulatory Accounting Practices (RAP). Accounting rules and procedures approved by the Federal Home Loan Bank Board for use by savings institutions under the Board's jurisdiction. They may differ from generally accepted accounting principles (GAAP), and are adopted by the Board to achieve policy objectives.

Release. (1) The discharge of property from a mortgage lien. (2) A written statement that an obligation has been satisfied.

REO. See Real Estate Owned.

Reorganization. The altering of a firm's capital, organization, and management structure following a plan worked out during bankruptcy proceedings under Chapter 11. The objectives of a reorganization are to eliminate the cause of the failure, settle with creditors, and allow the firm to remain in business.

Replacement cost. The current cost of producing a similar building or piece of equipment equal in utility and quality to the building or equipment already existing.

Repudiation. A receivership's right to disaffirm or cancel its obligation to continue to perform executory contracts which are deemed burdensome.

Request for Expedited Relief. A written request submitted by an affected person in accordance with applicable receivership claim procedures. A request for Expedited Relief is not a claim under FSLIC administrative claims procedures.

Reserves. (1) That portion of current earnings set aside to take care of possible future losses or for other specified purposes. (2) The portion of deposits in transaction accounts that must be held by depository institutions in liquid form (vault cash or deposits in a Federal Reserve Bank). Such reserves may not be used for lending or investing. The reserve ratio for transaction accounts or nonpersonal time deposits in all depository institutions (including commercial banks, savings banks, savings and loan associations, and credit unions) is set by the Board of Governors of the Federal Reserve System.

Review Committees. Committees established by the FSLIC to review and approve receivership asset business plans, and amendments thereto, including the amount established for each asset as the NRV.

Right of redemption. A right provided by law in some states permitting a mortgagor to reclaim foreclosed property by making full payment of the mortgage debt, including interest and fees, or the foreclosure sales price. The redemption period is for a specified period of time.

Savings account. An account maintained by a customer with a depository institution for the purpose of accumulating funds over a period of time. Funds deposited in a savings account may be withdrawn only by the account owner or a duly authorized agent, or on the owner's nontransferable order. The account may be owned by one or more persons.

Savings and loan association. An association of savers and borrowers formally established to accept deposits and make loans, primarily on residential real estate. An association may be organized as a mutual or a stock association. A mutual association is owned by its depositors and borrowers. A stock association is owned by its shareholders.

Savings association. A financial intermediary that accepts savings from the public and invests those savings primarily in residential mortgage loans. The association may be either a mutual or stock institution and may be federally or state chartered. Savings associations are also called savings and loan associations, building and loan associations, co-operative banks, or homestead societies.

Savings bank. A financial intermediary that accepts savings deposits. It invests these funds in loans primarily for commercial and residential real estate, investments in government and high quality corporate bonds, and blue chip stock. Savings banks may use up to 10 percent of their assets in commercial, business, or agricultural loans. These banks may be state or federally chartered and insured by the FSLIC or the FDIC.

Savings certificate. A document that is evidence of ownership of a savings account, typically an account in which a stated amount of funds is deposited for a fixed term.

Savings flows. The net increase or decrease in savings deposit balances of a savings institution during a specified period of time.

Savings institution. A financial intermediary established to promote thrift by accepting savings from members of a community. Savings institutions include both savings associations and savings banks. Savings institutions are also called thrift institutions.

Savings liability. The total amount of savings deposits entrusted to a depository institution by its depositors. It is the total amount of all savings account balances held by an institution, including earnings credited to such accounts, less redemptions and withdrawals.

Savings outflows. The net decrease over a period of time of savings account balances held by one or more savings institutions.

Scheduled items. Problem assets, which all FSLIC-insured savings institutions must report in a separate category. Scheduled items include slow real estate and consumer loans, real estate owned as a result of foreclosure, and real estate sold on contract or financed at a loan-to-value ratio greater than normally permitted. The amount listed as scheduled items is one measurement of the soundness of an institution's portfolio.

Seasoned mortgage. A mortgage that is at least one year old and for which principal and interest payments are being made on time.

Sealed bid. A sales process that requires submission of a written offer by a specified date.

Secondary mortgage market. A market through which existing mortgage loans are bought and sold to other lenders, to government or private agencies, or to investors. Mortgage loans are originated in the primary market and sold in the secondary market.

Security agreement. A document or section of a note that contains a description of the loan collateral. It establishes the lender's rights to the collateral in the event of default on the loan.

Seller's market. A market condition in which demand for a product or service exceeds available supply, resulting in higher prices favoring the seller. Opposite of buyer's market.

Service corporation. A corporation owned by one or more savings institutions that engages in business activities reasonably related to a savings institution. All activities must be approved by the Bank Board.

Solvency. The condition that exists when liabilities amount to less than total assets, thus providing the ability to pay debts.

Solvent. The state of being able to meet expenses and pay debts.

Special representative. The person designated by resolution of the FHLBB as having the power and authority to act in the name and on behalf of the receiver.

Special warranty deed. A form of real property ownership transfer used by FDIC and FSLIC receiverships whereby the FDIC/FSLIC as seller warrants good title to a property only from the date the FDIC/FSLIC as receiver took ownership. No warranties are made by the FDIC/FSLIC prior to legal acquisition of the asset. Prior ownership is guaranteed by title policy.

Specie. Coined money.

State-chartered association. A savings institution that has received its operating charter from a state regulatory authority and must conform to state law under which it is examined and supervised.

Stock association. A savings and loan association which sells stock to raise capital. It is owned by those who buy its stock, called shareholders, and they may share in profits earned by the association. See mutual association.

Subsidiary. An organization controlled by another organization or company.

Supervisory agent. An official at one of the Federal Home Loan Banks who has lawful authority delegated by the Federal Home Loan Bank Board to carry out the enforcement of laws and regulations dealing with the operation of savings institutions. The president of each District Bank is traditionally designated the Bank's principal supervisory agent.

Supervisory merger. A consolidation of savings institutions arranged by the Federal Home Loan Bank Board. A weak insolvent institution is merged into a strong institution with financial assistance from the Federal Savings and Loan Insurance Corporation (FSLIC).

Takeover. The legal act of transferring the assets of a defaulted FSLIC-insured institution into a receivership.

Tangible asset. Personal property that can be perceived by the senses (e.g., land, fixed improvements, furnishings, and merchandise).

Tax lien. A government claim against real property for unpaid taxes.

Term loan. A loan with a maturity of usually three to five years, during which time interest is paid but no payments to reduce principal are made. The entire principal is due and payable at the end of the loan term.

Thrift industry. All of the operating financial institutions that primarily accept deposits from individual savers and lend funds for home mortgages. These include savings and loan associations, savings banks, and credit unions.

Thrift institution. The general term for savings banks, savings and loan associations, and credit unions.

Thrifts. Another term for thrift institutions.

Time deposits. A deposit of funds in a savings institution under an agreement stipulating that (a) the funds must be kept on deposit for a stated period of time, or (b) the institution may require a minimum period of notification before a withdrawal is made.

Title. (1) The ownership right to property, including the right to possession. (2) The document or instrument constituting evidence of such an ownership right.

Title binder. A written evidence of temporary title insurance coverage in force for a limited period of time, which must be replaced by a permanent policy.

Title company. A business firm that examines real property titles and reports their findings as to the legal status of such titles. It issues insurance policies to indemnify the owner and lender against financial loss resulting from unknown title defects or prior claims against the property.

Title defect. Any fact, circumstance, or lawful right that could successfully claim all or part of a property or could challenge the ownership of the property.

Title insurance. The insurance that protects both the lender and the homeowner (borrower) against loss resulting from any defects in the title or claims against a property that were not uncovered in the title search, and that are not specifically listed as exemptions to the coverage on the title insurance policy.

Title report. A written statement by a title guarantee company that sets forth the condition of title to a specified piece of real estate as of a certain date.

Title search. A review of public records to determine whether there are any claims or defects in the current owner's title to real estate.

Treasury bill (T-bill). A short-term debt obligation issued by the U.S. Treasury at a discount under competitive bidding, with a maturity of up to one year. The bills are issued payable to the bearer only, and are sold at a minimum face value of $10,000.

Treasury bond. A Federal government debt obligation ordinarily payable to the bearer. It is issued at par with maturities of more than five years and with interest payable semiannually.

Treasury certificate. A U.S. Treasury security, usually issued at par with a specified rate of interest and a maturity of one year or less. It is issued payable to the bearer and sold in minimum amounts of $1,000.

Treasury note. A debt obligation of the U.S. Treasury, usually issued payable to the bearer with a fixed maturity of not less than one year nor more than seven years. It is issued at par, with a specific interest return payable semiannually.

Treasury securities. Interest-bearing debt obligations of the U.S. government that are issued by the Treasury. This means of borrowing money meets government expenditures not covered by tax revenues. Marketable Treasury securities include bills, notes, and bonds.

Trustee. (1) A person to whom the title of property has been conveyed for the immediate or eventual benefit of another. (2) The legal title holder and controller of funds in a trust account established under a trust agreement for the benefit of another.

Underwrite. (1) To sign one's name at the end of a document, thus signifying agreement or concurrence with the contents of the document. (2) To assume risk and liability for specified events in return for a fee. An insurance company, by signing a policy, becomes the policy's underwriter, thereby assuming the risk of being liable for losses if events specified in the policy occur. (3) In mortgage lending, the act of assessing the risk of a loan and matching it to an appropriate rate of interest and term. (4) To guarantee the sale of a new issue of securities, usually by a securities dealer or a syndicate of dealers.

United States League of Savings Institutions. A national organization representing the thrift industry.

Vacancy factor. A measurement of gross rental income loss due to vacancy and noncollection of rent. The rate is expressed as a percentage, and is calculated by dividing lost rental income (from vacancy and noncollection) into total potential gross rental income (including income from other rental units and the lost income).

Vendor. A seller of property, goods, or services.

Vest. (1) To confer the right of immediate or future possession and use of property. (2) A designation of ownership or possession of property. (3) A designation of the endowment of rights, power or authority.

Vested interest. A fixed interest in tangible or intangible property. The right of possession, use, and enjoyment may be postponed until some future date or until the happening of some event.

Waiver. The voluntary relinquishment of a right to one's own property or to a claim against another's property, or to any other legally enforceable right.

Warranty deed. A deed in which the seller warrants that the title to the real estate to be sold is good and salable from the property's date of origin to the date of closing.

Withdrawal. A removal of funds from a savings account by the account's owner.

Without rights of survivorship. An account in which the joint tenancy ends upon the death of one of the parties.

Working capital. Liquid assets available for conducting the daily affairs of a business.

Workout agreement. A plan approved by borrower and lender by which a delinquent borrower can reschedule loan payments so that the entire outstanding principal is eventually repaid.

Wraparound mortgage. A financing device that permits an existing loan to be refinanced and new, additional money to be advanced at an interest rate between the rate charged on the old loan and the current market interest rate. The creditor combines or "wraps" the remainder of the old loan with the new loan at the intermediate rate. The borrower makes one payment to the new lender who in turn makes the monthly payments to the original lender. The amount of the wraparound mortgage is the total of the outstanding principal of the first mortgage (which remains in effect) and the additional funds advanced by the wraparound lender.

Writ. A written order, under the seal of government authority, issued by a court and directing an officer of the court to perform some act, or enjoining a party to do or refrain from doing some act.

Write-off. The accounting procedure used when an asset has been determined to be uncollectible and is therefore charged off as a loss. On the books, the amount is removed from the asset portion of a balance sheet and recorded as an expense item on the income statement.

Yield. (1) The return on an investment, expressed as a percentage of the price paid for it originally. If the investment, such as a security, is not owned, its yield is its return expressed as a percentage of its current market price. (2) Income derived from an investment in property. (3) To give up possession; to pay.

Zero coupon bond. A security sold at deep discount from its face value and redeemed at its full face value at maturity. These bonds pay no interest. Instead, the investor's return is the difference between the purchase price of the bond and its face value when redeemed. Since these bonds do not pay interest, there are no interest coupons attached to the bond document, hence the name "zero-coupon bond." Even though the yield is not paid until maturity, the return accrues and is taxable on a prorated basis each year of the bond's life.

INDEX

REO $TRATEGY
The Savings & Loan Crisis!
Where Do We Go From Here?

REO $TRATEGY is a quarterly update to *How To Profit From The S&L Crisis*. This "nuts and bolts" newsletter provides money-making information in the ever-changing arena of foreclosed real estate. It explains how YOU can profit from the FSLIC-FDIC merger, the Resolution Trust Corp. (RTC), and the Financial Institutions Reform, Recovery and Enforcement Act of 1989. In an easy to read format, you learn

- Who are the players
- What are the rules
- How to play the game

☐ Please enter my subscription to **REO $TRATEGY**. Enclosed is my check of $100* for this highly informative quarterly newsletter.

Please tape your business card or complete below:

Name _____

Company _____

Address _____

City/State/Zip _____

Phone _____ Amount Enclosed* _____

*Houston, Texas residents please add 8% sales tax. All other Texas residents add 7% sales tax.

MONEY-BACK GUARANTEE

We offer an ironclad, money-back guarantee that lets you cancel at anytime with a prorata refund. Act now . . .

Please enclose your check made payable to:
Wilchester Publishing Company
P.O. Box 820874
Houston, Texas 77282-0874